Your Ultimate Comeback

How To Get Up When Life Knocks You Down

By

Rob Yanok

Book Cover Design: Ink Sharia Creative Studio

Edited By: Tricia Yanok

Author Photo by Robb Shirey, www.robbshirey.com

Author's custom sportcoat by Shawn Ricardo of Vincent & West Custom Clothier

vincentandwest.com

Printing and/or ordering information: amazon.com or robyanok.com

What People Are Saying

Ever find yourself needing a little encouragement and motivation to get you through the day? Maybe things haven't gone the way you planned in life or you feel like you've missed your moment. Well then, "Your Ultimate Comeback" is just for YOU! Rob has an amazing way of getting you back into the game of life with positive, practical, life-changing, EVERYDAY wisdom. His stories motivate you to stand up tall and face the day with a successful mindset. He builds hope in the reader that it's not about how many times you fall, but how many times you get back up! This is exactly the kind of book I LOVE to read. I am confident, no matter what age you are or what season of life you are in, you will thoroughly enjoy this book!

April Osteen Simons
Hope-Coach/Motivational

The ability to rebound from setbacks is the key to a successful life. Rebounding takes determination, effort, and a tenacious work ethic, but first, it requires the right mindset. In his book, Your Ultimate Comeback, Rob Yanok uses personal experiences and proven strategies to show how to develop the mindset needed to stand back up.

Dr. Dave Martin, Your Success Coach and
author of The 12 Traits of the Greats

A brilliant reminder to reframe the way you think about rejection. Rob reminds us to see it as a gift—a blessing in disguise. What is revolutionary is the transformation in your life when you commit to applying these ideas. I know firsthand—the results of your efforts WILL transform your life! Don't believe me? Try it for yourself, and find out! Your Ultimate Comeback is the guide you need, and it is already in your hands.

Simon T. Bailey, 40 Million views of his viral video on Facebook/Goalcast

---

"I love Rob Yanok! To be around this guy is to feel his enthusiasm for life, faith and people. And to be around his writing is the same as I feel when I'm around him. Reading this book will fill you with faith, life and hope for yourself and others around you as well."

Matt Keller; Founding and Lead Pastor of Next Level Church in Fort Myers, FL, Author of God of the Underdogs, and The Key To Everything

---

"Finding Success in Failure," what an empowering and amazing concept. Most would find this to be an oxymoron, but in my 17 years of ministering to professional football players, I have found this mindset to be absolutely true!

Rob's statement, "You cannot correct a problem you are not willing to face, but by the grace of God, you can turn your failure into victory," aptly details one of the biggest hurdles that most people face–fear of failure. The fear of failure can often stop people from realizing that failure does not disqualify them from their purpose. Therefore, it does not disqualify them from receiving God's grace to turn a failure into His victory!

I believe that this key, along with the many other amazing revelations in this book, will allow those who are bold enough to believe that as long as there is still time on the clock, they can win. Even when they're down, they will never be out!

Pastor Ted Winsley
Chaplain to the Super Bowl Champion Philadelphia Eagles!
Founder and Senior Pastor of the Family Church of Voorhees, New Jersey

---

"I wish I had read "Your Ultimate Comeback" sooner! The life of a professional soccer player is exactly the ability to over come challenges on a daily basis. I've always thought the true character of a man is not how he has failed but how he overcame the challenges in his life. Rob Yanok lives the principles in this book on a daily basis and everyone should touch base with their own grit and read "Your Ultimate Comeback."

Steve Clark
Professional Soccer Player
Goalkeeper, Portland Timbers

A Man Is Not A Loser Based Upon How Many Times He's Been Knocked Down... Loser Never Becomes His Name Until He Refuses To Get Back Up... In "Your Ultimate Comeback" Rob Lays Out For All Of Us The Strategy Necessary To Keep Getting Back Up, No matter What The Odds... Thank You Rob For This Book... It Will Be A Handbook For All Of Us Who Are Serious About "Winning In Life"...

Dr. Robb Thompson, CEO of Robb Thompson Coaching; Author of over 30 best-selling books

---

"Rob brilliantly reminds us to stop counting the number of times we fall down and to start counting the number of times we get up. An inspirational read for keeping our faith, building our resiliency and rising each & every day to maximize our potential."

Amy K Hutchens, International award-winning speaker & author

I named my ministry, Heart of David Ministry. You see, when I examined David's life, a life that had a lot of good, and a lot of bad, I realized it's our heart that God judges. You see, the same David who killed Goliath, who won battle after battle, and eventually became king of Israel, was just a man, and, like all men, a sinner. David committed adultery, lied in an attempt to cover it up, and had the husband of the woman he sinned with, killed in battle! Yet God said of David, "He is a man after my own heart"! WOW! How could God say that about David? Here's why.

He knew David, in spite of his sins and weaknesses, and no matter how many times he fell, he would always GET BACK UP! God knew David's heart, and at his core, he loved God and would never stop getting up! Thanks pastor Rob for this great reminder to us all! It was both challenging and refreshing to me. I think any honest man or woman who reads it, will think the same. We gotta keep getting up!!!

Ted Dibiase, Former WWE Hall Of Fame professional wrestler, Ordained Minister, & President of Heart of David Ministry

---

Your Ultimate Comeback is like a "plug in charger" for the psyche and the soul. Rob's simple yet impactful messages will recharge even the most depleted person. Everyone suffers through periods of doubt, times of failure and the uncertainty of how—or if—they can "pick themselves up and try again." These are the people who will benefit most from Your Ultimate Comeback.

The practical advice in this book is nicely balanced with the constant reminder of the importance of God's role in a person's life. This book can be literally a life-saver for a person who is deep in despair. It can also be the inspiration for a person who needs a dose of hope and faith. Share it widely. You will be doing a favor to everyone who reads it. God knows that too.

John Mariotti, the President/CEO & Founder of The Enterprise Group, a best selling author, former

President of Huffy Bicycles and Rubbermaid Office Products Group

---

Many nuggets of wisdom in this well written book. Rob reminds us not confuse Failure with being a Failure, we all fail on the road to success. I throughly enjoyed and reminded that it's OK to fail, it's OK to get knocked down but the joy is getting back up not giving up and realizing we all have the ability to be successful in life. Thank you for the reminder and inspiration! Kudos my friend!

Marc Mero
Former WCW & WWE Wrestling Champion & America's #1 School Presenter

---

"Be encouraged! Your best days are still ahead! With conversational warmth and practical insights, Rob has motivated me to fail forward, to persevere, and to make a much-needed comeback. With targeted tips, Rob will inspire you to develop the mental moxie you'll need to live a thriving, victorious, successful life."

Dr. Dave White, Success Life Coach, Entrepreneur, Pastor, NCAA Men's Basketball Lead Official

---

"This book is the loudest, most aggravating "written alarm clock" ever written! Whether you want to stay down or not, Rob Yanok's insight and carefully crafted layout motivates

you to GET UP! This book is equivalent to 110,000 people in a football stadium yelling "GET BACK UP. YOU CAN DO IT!"

Roy Hall, Former Ohio State Buckeye and NFL Indianapolis Colts Football Player, President of The Driven Foundation

---

"Rob Yanok kneels with his readers on the ground where dreams are shattered and all hope is gone. He speaks to broken champions and everyone who struggles to see a better tomorrow. This book is a halftime speech that will give you goosebumps and a strategy for getting up to win at life again, like you know you can!"

Dr. Chuck Balsamo, Pastor, Author, Pro Speaker and Personal Development Coach.

Table of Contents

Dedicated To

My Grandma June Snyder (1930-2018) When she was faced with the reality of death, said to us, " Todaloo, I'm here today, Gone tomorrow, but I Shall Arise". Thank you for your extraordinary example, faithfulness, love, cooking, caring, and most of all the prayers you prayed for all of us. We miss you everyday Bubba June!

and

Michael P. Friend, My Uncle, My Mentor, My Friend, My Coach, and My Pastor. The ultimate encourager, hope dealer, and believer in people who preached a sermon in the early 1980's that changed my life forever, "I Shall Arise".

"While you were feeling the sting of your SETBACK, God is preparing your COMEBACK!" Tim Storey

Why I Wrote this Book

"There is no sense in punishing your future self for the mistakes of your past. Forgive yourself, grow from it, and then let it go."

Melanie Koulouris

We make mistakes. We fall. We make stupid decisions. We lose. We fail. We feel condemned. Shamed. Discouraged. Depressed. These circumstances can be quite over-whelming for us. Trust me I know. I have made my share. The last few years have been the most difficult in my entire life, spiritually, emotionally, personally, financially, and relationally. I can honestly admit that some were my fault. I was not thinking right. I made the wrong decision. I hit the ground hard. Also, some were because of others. People can be toxic. They can be mean-spirited, selfish, arrogant, and downright nasty. In other situations, well, circumstances just happened.

Mistakes, failures, and falling are not who we are. It is only an event in our life. It does not define us. We all feel like a colossal failure at times when these things happen. We disappoint the people we love the most. Sometimes we get into a dark place that seems challenging to get through. A failed marriage, a relationship gone wrong, a struggling business that doesn't survive, struggling with finances that result in bankruptcy, and even the death of a dream.

We all make mistakes and bad decisions from time to time. The results of those situations tear us up inside. We feel paralyzed and held back. It is never easy. Sometimes resulting in us being locked in a prison of guilt, humiliation, self-doubt, regret, and shame. Do not make it your story. Pick up the broken pieces and make your life a mosaic.

The good news is that we can rise above all our setbacks, mistakes, and failures. We really can experience the ultimate comeback. That is why I wrote this book. It is not a question of "If" you fall, but "When" you fall. We should never be quick to judge or criticize. But to be compassionate, kind, restoring, believing, and hopeful that things change and even people change.

You may be in a situation or have come to a test where the darkness dominates the landscape. Morning always comes. The morning sunlight will soon govern the night. You have to get up and tell yourself you can do this! Don't you dare give up on this life. Not tonight. Not tomorrow. Not ever. One's life can be uniquely challenging sometimes, and during our darkest moments, we have all desperately looked for an answer to our problems. CS Lewis once said, "You can't go back and change the beginning, but you can start where you are and change the ending." Every morning we get a chance to be different. A chance to change. A chance to be better. A chance to get back up. Your past is your past. Leave it there. Your experience is your ultimate comeback. Remember success is what happens after you have survived all your mistakes.

Coaching, counseling, mentoring, and even helping people is never easy. But it is necessary for ongoing success in life, relationships, and business. I wish for this book to encourage you, give you hope, and inspire you. I hope it motivates you to look at your circumstance differently to realize it is not the end but the beginning of something new. I hope you find the wisdom to apply principles, ideas, and concepts to make your life extraordinary. Go ahead and highlight the points that speak to you. Keep this book near you, so when you find yourself knocked down in life, you can go ahead and pick this book back up, read it, renew your mindset, and be refreshed, revived, restored, and recovered.

Chapter 1

Everyone Gets Knocked Down

Rejoice not over me, O my enemy; when I fall, I shall rise; when I sit in darkness, the Lord will be a light to me.

Micah 7:8 ESV

"It's not whether you get knocked down, it's whether you get up."

Vince Lombardi #robberbs

If you fall, try to land on your back because if you can LOOK UP, you can GET UP!"

Les Brown #robberbs

An ancient prophet once said, *"When I fall, I shall arise..."* He is explaining to the world that he had fallen. The enemy had knocked him down. I do not know the exact details and what happened or what he did. All I know is that he had fallen. All of us, no matter who we are, have fallen at different times in our lives. We have missed it. We have failed. We have blown it. Well, we have lost. Micah was making it very clear to the enemy, or the thing that caused him to fall, he boldly declared, "I shall arise," I will get back up! The worst thing anyone can do is to refuse to get back up. There comes a time in your life when you finally have to decide that falling is not the end of your story. You fell, but failure doesn't define who you are. It is just an event in your life, and it happens to everyone.

Mike Tyson vs. Buster Douglas, billed as Tyson Is Back!, was a professional boxing match that occurred at the Tokyo Dome on February 11, 1990. The event is historically significant, as the then-undefeated, undisputed heavyweight champion Tyson lost by a knockout to the 42–1 underdog[1][2] Douglas. The fight is widely considered one of the biggest upsets in sports history.

The last 10 seconds of the 8th round, Tyson, was backed onto the ropes and landed a big right uppercut sending Douglas to the canvas. In times past, whoever got knocked out by Tyson never got back up. It seemed as though Douglas was down for the count, but as the referee started the countdown to the last second and it would be all over, Douglas got up after a 9-second countdown.

In the tenth round, Tyson pushed forward to fight, but he was still seriously hurting from the accumulation of punishment given throughout the match. As Tyson walked forward, Douglas measured him with a few jabs before landing a devastating uppercut that snapped Tyson's head upward, stopping Tyson in his tracks. As Tyson began to reel back from the uppercut, Douglas immediately followed with four punches to the head, knocking Tyson down for the first time in his career. In a famous scene, Tyson fumbled for his mouthpiece on the canvas before sticking one end in his mouth with the other end hanging out. The champion attempted to make it back to his feet to continue fighting, but referee Octavio Meyran counted him out. Buster Douglas thus became the new undisputed heavyweight champion, and the fight became one of the biggest upsets in boxing history.

Mohammad Ali said, "You don't lose if you get knocked down, You lose if you stay down." Douglas got up even though he got knocked down. What would have become of him if he had not gotten back up? Well, he would not have beaten Mike Tyson and become the Heavyweight Champion of the World.

There is an ancient fact found in 2 Corinthians 4:8-9 ESV, Paul was motivating and inspiring the Corinthian Church and told them, *"We are afflicted in every way, but not crushed; perplexed, but not driven to despair; persecuted, but not forsaken; struck down, but not destroyed;"* In other words, this is a human world and falling is just a part of life. Falling does not have to destroy us. Paul wanted them to know that falling happens to everyone. It is a part of life. So you have to get up! You do not drown by falling into the water; you drown by staying there.

Getting Knocked Down is a Fact of Life

Jesus said in John 16:33, *"I have told you these things, so that in me you may have peace. In this world, you will have trouble (tribulation). But take heart! I have overcome the world."* The word tribulation means, Pressure, Oppression, stress, anguish, adversity, affliction, crushing, squeezing, and distress. In life, these things Jesus said would cause us to get knocked down. It just will happen. Getting knocked down in life is a given. It is a part of life, finances, business, and relationships. Getting up and moving forward is a choice.

Getting Knocked Down happens to everyone.

Life is no respecter of persons. There is a verse of scripture in Matthew 5:45 that says about God, "He causes his sun to rise on the evil and the good, and sends rain on the righteous and the unrighteous. God is saying both good and bad things can happen to bad and good people. That is life. Everyone experiences some form of setback, failure, adversity, or some loss in their lifetime. It happens many times without notice. When it happens, the result is usually, anxiety, stress, frustration, disappointment, fear, sadness, and even hopelessness.

Here are some prime examples of famous people who got knocked down. JK Rowling was turned down by multiple publishers for years while living out of her car. If she had stayed down, there would be no Harry Potter. What if Walt Disney quit after his Theme Park concept was trashed and turned down 302 times by Banks. There would be no Disney Land. Howard Schultz, CEO of Starbucks was turned down by banks 242 times. If he never got back up, there would be no Starbucks today. Then there is Col. Sanders, founder of Kentucky Fried Chicken, he was rejected 1009 times for his Chicken recipe and contemplated suicide. These are just some examples of some successful people who in spite of getting knocked down and disappointed, Got back up! Getting knocked down happens to everybody.

Apostle Paul was knocked down in his attempt to move the church forward. He said in I Thessalonians 2:18 NIV - *"For we wanted to come to you—certainly I, Paul, did, again and again—but Satan blocked (Hindered) our way."* When a child is learning how to walk and falls 50 times, They never think to themselves, "Maybe this is not for me." They get back up!

Getting Knocked Down Won't Last Forever

Charlie Chaplin once said, "Nothing is permanent in this wicked world, not even our troubles." Thank God for that. Although sometimes it seems like it does last forever. I remember growing up watching WWE Wrestling. After the announcer introduced each wrestler, he would end it by saying, "This match is for a ten-minute time limit." This statement meant the match could only last ten minutes before someone would win, lose, or it would be a draw.

The Apostle Paul wanted us to know that our light and momentary troubles are achieving for us an eternal glory that far outweighs them all (2 Corinthians 4:17). After reading that I was like, what? Light? Momentary? Doesn't he realize that my battle has felt like forever and it's wearing me out? Have you ever felt that way? But he was correct. It won't last forever. You and I are going to outlast the battle. Remember, even the darkest hour only lasts sixty minutes. So we need to get up and go on!

Getting Knocked Down Can Be Good For Us

This statement is a tough one to swallow. Getting knocked down can be useful for us? Yes, even though none of us ever think that when we have gone through it. CS Lewis once said, "God who foresaw your tribulation, has specifically armed you to go through it, not without pain, but without stain." I will cover failure in another chapter, but the reality is sometimes you have to get knocked down lower than ever expected, to stand up taller than you ever were. One's faith, tenacity, and endurance are always tested by hardships, disappointments, and difficulties.

If you have any faith in God, Paul was telling us in Romans 8:28 NIV, *"And we know that in all things God works for the good of those who love him, who[a] have been called according to his purpose."* In other words, If you love God, everything in life is working for your good, even getting knocked down. You do not see that when it is happening. You look at these things as destructive. Some people go through the furnace of trouble, and it burns them, others go in it, and the experience builds them. If you have ever been knocked down, get back up! Do not allow it to destroy you. Allow it to strengthen you.

On New Year's Day, 1929, Georgia Tech played the University of California in the Rose Bowl. In that game, a man named Roy Riegels recovered a fumble for California. Somehow, he became confused and started running 65 yards in the wrong direction. One of his teammates, Benny Lom, outdistanced him and downed him just before he scored for the opposing team. When California attempted to punt, Tech blocked the kick and scored a safety which was the ultimate margin of victory.

That strange play came in the first half, and everyone who was watching the game was asking the same question: "What will Coach Nibbs Price do with Roy Riegels in the second half?" The men filed off the field and went into the dressing room. They sat down on the benches and on the floor, all but Riegels. He put his blanket around his shoulders, sat down in a corner, put his face in his hands, and cried like a baby.

If you have played football, you know that a coach usually has a great deal to say to his team during halftime. That day Coach Price was quiet. No doubt he was trying to decide what to do with Riegels. Then the timekeeper came in and announced that there were three minutes before playing time. Coach Price looked at the team and said, "Men, the same team that played the first half will start the second." The players got up and started out, all but Riegels. He did not budge. The coach looked back and called to him again; still, he didn't move. Coach Price went over to where Riegels sat and said, "Roy, didn't you hear me? The same team that played the first half will start the second." Then Roy Riegels looked up, and his cheeks were wet with a strong man's tears. "Coach," he said, "I can't do it to save my life. I've ruined you, I've ruined the University of California, I've ruined myself. I couldn't face that crowd in the stadium to save my life." Then Coach Price reached out and put his hand on Riegel's shoulder and said to him: "Roy, get up and go on back; the game is only half over." And Roy Riegels went back, and those Tech men will tell you that they have never seen a man play football as Roy Riegels played that second half. (Haddon W. Robinson, Christian Medical Society Journal)

You must always remember, the person who falls and gets back up is so much stronger than the one who never fell. So don't hope your life was good, don't wish it will get better. Get up and make your life extraordinary. Your story isn't over yet. You have got so much more to give and share with the world. No need to keep beating yourself up. Everyone gets knocked down. Everyone falls. I know you are hurting, I know you're struggling to make sense of your life and maybe your even trying to figure out how the heck you ended up on the ground.

Your current situation is not your final destination. Your failures, mistakes, and falling do not have to define you. Your life, your success, your story, is still being written. Get back up! It's not over. Tim Storey said, "While you were feeling the sting of your SETBACK, God is preparing your COMEBACK!" It is far from over, and you do not have to give in and give up because certain things did not work out. Again, get up, smile, be thankful that you get another chance to re-define and re-create your life.

Chapter 2

Finding Success in Failure

"I have not failed. I've just found 10,000 ways that won't work."

Thomas A. Edison #robberbs

"You have to be able to accept failure to get better."

LeBron James #robberbs

"I wasn't afraid to fail. Something good always comes out of failure."

Anne Baxter #robberbs

Failure is such a relative term. Sooner or later in life everyone experiences failure, disappointments, and setbacks. I can honestly say I have failed more times than succeeded. I have failed many times as a husband to my wife, as a father to my children, as a pastor to my church, and as an entrepreneur in my business. But real winners are not afraid of losing. Failure is part of the process of success. People who avoid failure also avoid success.

Over the years I have had my share of failures and successes. Failing doesn't make you a loser. Achieving success doesn't make you successful. I know many of people who have hit rock bottom, only to climb out and achieve greatness, and massive success. What you learn from all the setbacks in life and how you get back up after being knocked down is so much more important in the long run than the actual battle you face. Successful people know that it is possible to be developed by failure, instead of destroyed. To look at it positively as a learning experience that makes you stronger and better prepared to overcome any future challenges.

The only real failure we make is the one from which we learn nothing. The longer you live, the more you will have to deal with failure. When you do fail, don't give up. The key to overcoming failure is to recognize that it can be beneficial. God wants us to learn from our failures. He especially wants us to learn not to make the same mistake again. We need to face our weaknesses and accept personal responsibility for our actions. You cannot correct a problem you are not willing to meet. But, by the grace of God, you can turn your failure into victory.

Maybe you feel like the "Would Be Bank Robber." He felt like a failure! Everything he attempted seemed to turn out wrong. He began to fantasize about being rich. He would do the one thing he could do to make the most money in the briefest period. He would take up the occupation of bank robbing. The would-be bank robber began to plan his strategy. He sat up late at night working on detailed plans, drawing sketches and going over steps he would take in robbing the bank. But he could never seem to get around to robbing the bank. He would plan each night, but when morning came, his anxiety paralyzed him, again. One night he determined that his mind was made up. Regardless of his feelings, he would force himself to rob the bank the next morning. The next morning an anxiety attack paralyzed him again. Finally, he came through it and

forced himself to get into his car and go to the bank. The reluc-
tant bank robber sat in the car in the parking lot from 10 a.m.
to 1 p.m. trying to force himself out of the car. Finally, he got
out of the car and went into the bank. At the teller's window,
he handed the teller his pistol. He stuck his brown paper bag
in her face and said, "Don't stick with me, this is a mess-up."

Success and Failure Defined

Success defined is the favorable or prosperous termination
of attempts or endeavors, the accomplishment of one's goals.
The attainment of wealth, position, honors, or the like. Failure
defined is the state or condition of not meeting a desirable or
intended objective, and may be viewed as the opposite of success. Remember this, everyone succeeds, and everyone fails.
The thing that will distinguish your ultimate success from any
of your failures is what you do with them. A failure is only a
failure if you decide it is. Take it and learn, learn, learn, it will
be your success and your win.

How do you respond when you have failed? Do you avoid
taking risks for fear of failure? A successful person is not one
who never fails. A successful person is one who learns from
his/her mistakes and failures and grows from them. Be developed by failure, instead of destroyed by it.

At seven years old his family lost their home. He went to
work to support them. Nine years old he was a backward, shy
little boy. Then his mother died. At 22 years old he lost his job
as a store clerk and could not fulfill his dream of going to law
school. He did not even have enough education. At 23 years
old he became a partner in a small store, but three years later his business partner died leaving him a massive debt that
took years to repay. At 28 years old, he proposed marriage

to a young lady he had seen for four years. She said, "No." He had earlier been in love with a young lady and she with him, but it ended in heartache when she died. Then at 37 years old, he was elected to Congress on his third try. At 39 years old, he failed to be re-elected and ended up having a nervous breakdown. At 41 years old, in the midst of a miserable marriage, his four-year-old son died. He was rejected, at 42 years old, for a position of Land Officer. At 45 years old, he ran for the Senate and lost. He was defeated, at 47 years old in his nomination for Vice President. At 49 years old, he ran for the Senate again and lost. Add to this an endless barrage of criticism, false rumors, and misunderstandings. At 51 years old, he was elected President of the United States. His second term in office was cut short by an assassin's bullet. As this man lay dying .... Edwin Stanton, one of his former opponents and bitterest enemies, said: "There lies the most perfect ruler of men the world has ever seen... Now he belongs to the ages." .... This man's name: Abraham Lincoln.

Abraham Lincoln is rated as one of America's best presidents, but had many setbacks before being elected president in 1860. This example was meant to show that even one who has failures became president because he did not give up. Remember your future is always greater than your failure.

Famous Successful Failures

You are not the only one that failed. Everyone experiences failure. It doesn't matter how many times you fall or fail. Champions get back up. Because what they have yet to accomplish is more important than lying in defeat or self-pity. Winston Churchill once said, "Success consists of going from failure to failure without loss of enthusiasm." All human beings fail. God is fully aware of your limitations. The Scripture says, For he knows our frame; he remembers that we are dust (Psalm 103:14). God knows our limitations, and we must accept them as well. True success is not avoiding failure but learning what to do with it.

In his day, Babe Ruth, with his reputation as the King of Home Runs, also came the title of the King of Strikeouts. Alongside his 714 career home runs stood a legacy of 1,330 strikeouts—a strikeout was only a momentary if melodramatic, setback. He said "Every strike brings me closer to the next home run," It is better to attempt things and fail than never to attempt anything because you are afraid to fail. You never learn the limits of our ability until you reach the point of total failure. Thomas Edison tried over five thousand different types of light-bulb filaments before he found one that would work. His willingness to endure many failures gave us the modern electric light.

Whenever you attempt to do something and fail, you end up doing something else or producing something else. You have not failed; you have created some other result. The two most important questions to ask are: "What have I learned?" and "What have I done?" Failure is only a word that human beings use to judge a given situation. Instead of fearing failure, one should learn that failures, mistakes, and errors are the way you learn and the way you grow. Many of the world's greatest successes have determined how to fail his/her way to success.

You all know the names. You have heard them time and time again. But what most people don't know is just how they failed before they succeeded. The consensus of success in the arts, entertainment, or business doesn't take into account personal struggles. All we see are the personification of that success through whatever outlet we happen to come by it. While you struggle day-in and day-out towards the fulfillment of your hopes and your dreams, know this: "If there is no struggle there is no progress." Although Fredrick Douglas might have conveyed this statement more than 150 years ago, it is a theme that has been evident since the dawn of time. Organisms, both small and large, have always fought for survival, struggling for progress across all spectrums of life.

Here is a list of some famous people who failed before they succeeded. These were people who did not give up in the face of their struggles. They are people that persevered. They pushed through their present-day limitations, had breakthroughs, and whose names have become synonymous with success in their respective fields of study and work:

Albert Einstein: Most of us take Einstein's name as synonymous with genius, but he didn't always show such promise. Einstein did not speak until he was four and did not read until he was seven, causing his teachers and parents to think he was mentally disabled, slow and anti-social. Eventually, he was expelled from school and was refused admittance to the Zurich Polytechnic School. He attended a trade school for one year and then admitted to the University. He was the only one of his graduating class unable to get a teaching position because no professor would recommend him. One professor labeled him as the laziest dog they ever had in the university. The only job he was able to get was an entry-level position in a government patent office.

Oprah Winfrey: She had a rocky start in life. As the daughter of a teenaged low-income mother, her start was anything but glamorous. In her early years, Oprah recounts that not only were her living conditions rough, but she was always sexually abused, starting at the age of 9, by her cousin, uncle, and a family friend. At the age of 14, Oprah got pregnant, but her son died shortly after birth. However, at the age of 14, Oprah was sent to live with her father, Vernon, in Tennessee. He helped her focus on her schooling, and she was subsequently accepted on a full scholarship to Tennessee State University, majoring in communications. In high school, and in her first two years of college, Winfrey interned at a local radio station, helping to develop a foundation for a career in media. But, even after Oprah was hired on to a local television station for the news, things didn't go so smoothly. She was fired by the producer because she was "unfit for television," later taking a position with another station in Baltimore. Eventually, she hosted a local talk show named; People are Talking. Then, in 1983, Winfrey relocated to Chicago, to host a station's low-rated talk show called AM Chicago. Within a few months, the show went from last in the ratings, to higher than Donahue, which was the number one show at the time. Increased ratings caused the show to be renamed The Oprah Winfrey Show, which was syndicated across the country.

JK Rowling: She is one of the most inspirational success stories of our time. Many people just know her as the woman who created Harry Potter. But, what most people don't know is what she went through before reaching stardom. Rowling's life was not peaches and cream. She struggled tremendously.

In 1990, Rowling first had the idea for Harry Potter. She stated that the idea came "fully formed" into her mind one day while she was on a train from Manchester to London. She began writing furiously. However, later that year, her mother died after ten years of complications from Multiple Sclerosis. In 1992 she moved to Portugal to teach English where she met a man, married, and had a daughter. In 1993, her marriage ended in divorce, and she moved to Edinburgh, Scotland to be closer to her sister. At that time, she had three chapters of Harry Potter in her suitcase. Rowling saw herself as a failure at this time. She was jobless, divorced, penniless, and with a dependent child. Rowling suffered through bouts of depression, eventually signing up for government-assisted welfare. It was a difficult time in her life, but she pushed through the failures. In 1995 all 12 significant publishers rejected the Harry Potter script. But, it was a year later when a small publishing house, Bloomsbury, accepted it and extended a minimal £1500 advance. In 1997, the book was published with only 1000 copies, 500 of which not to libraries. In 1997 and 1998, the book won awards from Nestle Smarties Book Prize and the British Book Award for Children's Book of the Year. After that, it was one wild ride for Rowling. Today, Rowling has sold more than 400 million copies of her books and is considered to be the most successful woman author in the United Kingdom.

Bill Gates: Before Microsoft was born, Bill Gates suffered failure in business. Known today to be one of the wealthiest men in the world, Bill Gates's upper-middle-class family is a stark contrast from some of the other successful failures out there that didn't have well-off parents. However, Bill Gates did not rely on his family. His business acumen was second to none. But his first business was indeed a failure. Traf-O-Data was a partnership between Gates, Paul Gilbert, and Paul Allen. The goal of the business was to create reports for roadway engineers from raw traffic data.

The company did achieve a little bit of success by processing the raw traffic data to generate some income. But the machine that they had built to handle the data flopped when they tried to present it to a Seattle County, traffic employee. This business helped to set Gates and his partner Paul Allen up for major success with Microsoft. Although Gates failed at his first business, it did not discourage him from trying again. He did not want to give up because the sheer notion of business intrigued him. He was cleverly able to put together a company that revolutionized the personal computing marketplace. And we all know just how successful that was for him.

Thomas Edison: We have all heard the name before. This famous American failed over 10,000 times to invent a commercially viable electric light bulb, but he did not give up. When asked by a newspaper reporter if he felt like a failure and if he should give up, after having gone through over 9,000 failed attempts, Edison simply stated "Why would I feel like a failure? And why would I ever give up? I now know over 9,000 ways an electric light bulb will not work. Success is almost in my grasp."

Edison is also the same person whose teachers said he was "too stupid to learn anything," and fired from his first two employment positions for not being productive enough. However, Edison, through his failures, is also the greatest innovator of all time with 1,093 US patents to his name, along with several others in the UK, and Canada. He is someone who refused ever to give up, no matter what. It is said that in his early days, Edison attributed his success to his mother, who pulled him out of school and began to teach him herself. It is because of his mother, and how wholeheartedly she believed in him, that he did not want to disappoint her. His early fascination with chemical experiments and mechanical engineering paved the way for a future that was incredibly bright. His company, GE, is still one of the largest publicly traded firms in the world, continually innovating across virtually every spectrum.

Walt Disney: The man who has affected generations to come with his cartoon creations, was once considered a failure. Disney was fired by the editor in 1919 from his job at the Kansas City Star paper because he "lacked imagination and had no good ideas." However, the man who brought us

Mickey Mouse and a slew of other characters did not stop failing there.

Disney's first go at business landed in bankruptcy when he acquired an animation studio by the name of Laugh-O-Gram. The company was acquired because, at the time, Disney's cartoon creations had gained popularity in the Kansas City area. But, when he hired on salaried employees, he was unable to manage money, and the business wound up profoundly in debt. Subsequently, he filed for bankruptcy and moved to Hollywood, California. The early failures in Disney's life didn't dissuade him from moving forward. Of course, like anyone else, Disney's failures were a blow to the ego. Anyone that has to suffer through the torment of failure and bankruptcy knows how this feels. However, it also laid the foundation for a successful career. When he formed the Walt Disney Company, all of his past failures helped to pave the way for a successful business. Disney and the Walt Disney Company have touched the lives of millions across the globe. From cartoons to theme parks and animated movies, both children and adults now enjoy the fruits of Disney's labor. Had he given up, things would have been far different. But he persevered, even through bankruptcy.

Then what about Michael Jordan: Most people would not believe that a man often lauded as the best basketball player of all time was cut from his high school basketball team. Luckily, Jordan did not let this setback stop him from playing the game, and he has stated, "I have missed more than 9,000 shots in my career. I have lost almost 300 games. On 26 occasions I have been entrusted to take the game-winning shot, and I missed. I have failed over and over and over again in my life. And that is why I succeed." I love his tips for success: 1. Be positive 2. Be an optimist 3. Follow your dreams 4. Stop making excuses 5. FAIL YOUR WAY TO SUCCESS.

Failure is Unavoidable

Face the facts. You are human. No matter who you are, no matter what your walk of life, you will make mistakes. If you do not make mistakes, there could be something wrong with you!

Theodore Roosevelt said, "The only man who never makes a mistake is the man who never does anything." The simple reality is that failure is one of those ugly realities of life. A typical experience for all of us. Everyone has failed. So many notable individuals have failed in life more times than they have succeeded. You should never worry about failures. Worry about the chances you miss when you do not even try.

Understand that Failure is a moment in your life, not a monument.

Too many times when people fail, they erect a monument to their mistake and spend the rest of their lives re-living the event. To turn failure into success, take a moment and evaluate what went wrong, establish a new way of doing things, and then keep moving.

Failures only last as long as you allow them. Failure does not mean failure unless you refuse to learn from it. Ask yourself what lesson you need to learn so that you can move on.

Don't confuse Failure with being a Failure Remember: I am not a failure until I give up! The only way that failure can break you is if you let it. What you have to understand is that everybody fails. But not everyone gets back up and tries again. Realize that there is one significant difference between average and achieving people. How people see failures and deal with it impact every aspect of their lives.

Failure in life may look like a fact, but it is only an opinion. You have to look at failure differently. You have the potential to overcome failures, misfortunes, difficulties, all you have to do is to learn to fail forward.

Failure is Never the end....It is a New Beginning. If you have never failed at something, then you have not pushed yourself past your comfort zone. We all fail. Failure is a sign of life. Do not take failure as a sign of death.

Find the silver lining in the cloud of failure

Don't allow a failure to go unsearched. Learning from a mistake results in taking a significant step toward success. When you see your mistakes are you willing to change? When you change, you position yourself for success. People who win are not afraid of losing because they know that failure is part of the process of success and winning in this life. People who avoid failure also avoid success.

There is an Ancient Proverb that says, Blessed are those who find wisdom, those who gain understanding, Begin to see Failure as your friend. Although they may seem uncomfortable and painful at the time, you can turn them around to your benefit."No man ever became great or good except through many and great mistakes." Failure is simply an opportunity to learn.

Failures and mistakes can be a bridge, not a barricade

Thomas Edison invented the microphone, the phonograph, the incandescent light, the storage battery, talking movies, and more than 1000 other things. On December 1914 he had worked for ten years on a storage battery significantly straining his finances. This particular evening spontaneous combustion had broken out in the film room. Within minutes all the packing compounds, celluloid for records and film, and other flammable goods were in flames. Fire companies from eight surrounding towns arrived, but the heat was so intense and the water pressure so low that the attempt to douse the flames was futile. Everything was destroyed. Edison was 67.

With all his assets going up in a whoosh (although the damage exceeded two million dollars, the buildings were only insured for $238,000 because they were made of concrete and thought to be fireproof), would his spirit be broken? The inventor's 24-year old son, Charles, searched for his father. He finally found him, calmly watching the fire, his face glowing in the reflection, his white hair blowing in the wind. "My heart ached for him," said Charles. "He was 67—no longer a young man—and everything was going up in flames. When he saw me, he shouted, 'Charles, where's your mother?' When I told him I didn't know, he said, 'Find her. Bring her here. She will never see anything like this as long as she lives.'"

The next morning, Edison looked at the ruins and said, "There is great value in disaster. All our mistakes are burned up. Thank God we can start anew." Three weeks after the fire, Edison managed to deliver the first phonograph. "I have not failed. I've just found 10,000 ways that won't work." Vernon Sanders said, "Experience is a hard teacher because she gives the test first, and the lesson afterward."

Failure is a state of mind in so many ways, and we all fall victim to feeling defeated. Just because you've taken some hits does not mean you have lost. John Maxwell said, "Sometimes you will, and sometimes you learn." How you see losses and failures is more important than how you see the losses and failures themselves. Robert Kennedy once said, "Those who dare to fail miserably, can achieve greatly."

The Greatest Result of Failure is Education and Wisdom

"If you learn from defeat, you have not really lost." —Zig Ziglar

What you have to take away from failure is the lesson that failure gives you. Henry Ford once said, "Failure is the opportunity to begin again more intelligently." Failures are a part of life. If you do not fail, you do not learn. If you do not learn, you will never succeed. Never be afraid to fail. Be afraid of not learning from your mistakes.

A young man asked the old man, "What's the secret of your success?" Good decisions, he replied. How do you learn to make good decisions? You get that by experience. How do you get experience? By making bad decisions. Oscar Wilde once said, "Experience is simply the name we give our mistakes."

The biggest mistakes often yield the most significant lessons. Jim Rohn said, "Formal education will make you a living; self-education will make you a fortune." When you increase in learning, you will Increase in earning. The most valuable thing you can make is a mistake or a bad decision. You cannot learn anything from being perfect. The fact that you have failed is proof you are not finished. You do not drown by falling in the water; you drown by staying there. Ralph Waldo Emerson said, "The greatest glory in living lies not in never falling, but in rising every time we fall."

Sir Edmund Hillary who was attempting to scale Mt. Everest. He ended up losing one of his team members in a failed effort. He returned with a hero's welcome in London where a banquet was held in his honor and attended by all the powerful people of Great Britain. Behind the speaker's platform, they had hung a huge blown up photo of Mt. Everest. When Sir Edmund Hillary rose to receive the acclaim of this distinguished audience, he turned around, faced the picture and said… "Mt. Everest, you have defeated me… but I will return! And I will defeat you! Because you can't get any bigger… and I can!" Eventually, he did scale that vast Mountain and was the 1st man ever to do so.

Lewis Howes said, Failure is not painful if you see its feedback and the step to success. The greatest leaders and achievers have failed 10,000 more times then most people try. They know that failure is the secret to achieving their dreams. It is the prerequisite and elite schooling to give them the skills and grit to overcome the obstacles and pain in life that most people will never have the desire to endure. Look at failure as information teaching you the next step to take toward your desired dreams.

It is never easy to deal with the pain of failure, rejection, and disappointment, but you have to remember that what you are working towards and who you are is bigger than any single failure. Do not let your failures bury you. Let them Inspire you! Yesterdays failures can become today's success! Remember: Whoever counted you out, Cannot count! Never let success get to your head and never let failure get to your heart! Stay focused on your vision for life and learn to accept your failures and mistakes as lessons that allow you to further create your vision and dreams in life. Hillary Rodham Clinton said, "When you stumble, keep the faith. And when you are knocked down, get right back up and never listen to anyone who says you cannot or should not go on." Never let success go to your head and never let failure get to your heart.

Chapter 3

Faith...You Gotta Believe

The Mind is the limit. As long as the mind can envision the fact that you can do something, you can do it — as long as you really believe a 100%.

Arnold Schwarzenegger #robberbs

"If you can believe, all things are possible to him who believes."

Mark 9:23 (NIV)

"Sometimes life hits you in the head with a brick. Don't lose faith"

Steve Jobs #robberbs

Tony Robbins said, "All personal breakthroughs begin with a change in beliefs." Without faith nothing is possible. With it, nothing is impossible. Tug McGraw was 59 when he died of brain cancer on Jan. 5, 2004. His baseball legacy is well-known: The southpaw relief pitcher was a two-time All-Star and won two World Series rings. He began inspiring teammates with "Ya gotta believe" as a player on the New York Mets during their 1973 National League championship season. In

1974 he was traded to the Philadelphia Phillies, and he was still repeating the slogan in the clubhouse when the team made it to the Big Show in 1980.

During Game 6, McGraw struck out Kansas City Royal Willie Wilson for the final out of the Series. The photo of McGraw leaping in the air, his arms raised in victory, is as iconic in Philadelphia as the "Rocky" statue. McGraw also was known for his larger-than-life personality. A screwball pitcher, he wasn't ashamed to say he could be a screwball in life, too. He was quick with a quip –– once asked whether he preferred playing on grass or AstroTurf, he said, "I don't know. I never smoked any AstroTurf" –– and generous with his time. He autographed balls, replied to fan mail and generally seemed to relish life. As New York Times baseball writer Tyler Kepner noted in a 2004 appreciation piece, every kid who grew up around Philadelphia loved McGraw. "How could you not? Mike Schmidt hit home runs. Steve Carlton struck people out. Pete Rose smacked singles. Tug McGraw smiled all the time." He smiled because he believed. He believed inspire of circumstances. Voltaire once said concerning faith, "Faith consists of believing when it is beyond the power of reason to believe."

Faith and believing is the position that puts you above and sees you through all problems, defeats, and failures. Augustine said, "Faith is to believe what we do not see, and the reward of this faith is to see what we believe." You have to believe! You can't make a significant change for the better without some faith, hope, and belief. "Now faith is the assurance of things hoped for, the conviction of things not seen." Faith is an incredible strength, an extraordinary weapon of the soul, which allows us to persevere even when the present seems unbearable and the future uncertain. Bishop TD Jakes said, "Faith is the light that leads us out of darkness, and the map that guides our way.

The Greek word for faith is, in virtually every instance, the same word for belief. Although translators choose whether "faith" or "belief" is intended based on their understanding of the context of each passage, the meaning is usually much broader than either word alone.

Even in modern language, to believe in someone, something or some cause is to have faith in or trust that person, thing or movement—to believe it is true, just and worthy of one's support and involvement. In the same way, to have faith as it is defined in the Bible is to fully believe in—to have complete trust in—someone (God), to believe in and act on the truth of His Word (the Bible) and to live for the greatest of causes: salvation for all who believe in the coming Kingdom of God (Mark 1:14-15). Faith is belief. But do not make the age-old mistake of thinking that if you believe in God—that is, that He exists—you, therefore, have faith. Many hold on to this mistaken idea. One can say he/she believes in God; therefore, he/she thinks they have faith. There are plenty of "Christians" who believe in God but are so short on faith.

God Has No Limitations

A father was questioning Jesus' ability to cast a demon out of his child when Jesus responded with the following statement: In Mark 9:23 And Jesus said to him, "If you can? All things are possible to him who believes." What is meant by the words, 'All things are possible'? What exactly is included in the 'all things'? And looking at {them} Jesus said to them in Matthew 19:26 "With people this is impossible, but with God all things are possible." Matthew 19:26 Looking at them, Jesus said in Mark 10:27, *"With people, it is impossible, but not with God; for all things are possible with God."* Jesus continued to say in Mark 14:36, Then he said in Luke 1:37, *"For nothing will be impossible with God."*

If YOU can Believe, ALL THINGS ARE POSSIBLE!

The 'all things' means "ALL THINGS," and is limited to only those items that can be believed. Jesus is saying, "If you can believe it, then it is possible." The limitation is on our believing. Over-and-over again, a simple concept is communicated — 'There are no limitations with God, and the limitations that man received in the Great Fall are neutralized by his faith in God.' In effect, faith in the 'God of no limitations' takes away the limitations of man. This concept is not elevating man; it is elevating the blessing of God upon man. The source of the power is not a man but rather faith in God – "If you can believe it, it will happen." God is saying, "I have no limitations, if you can believe in me, I can do it." God gives us the power to get up!

Even if you can't figure it all out or explain God, there is an underlying belief that there is a God and you believe. The same thing with life, difficulties, and getting knocked down, You have to believe! Your circumstances can and will change. There is a better day coming and that you can get back up and move forward.

Faith comes in Can's & Doubt comes in Cant's

Henry Ford said, "If you believe you can, or if you believe you can't, you are right." That is so very true. He was talking about the power of belief. The more often than not, people will succeed not by their merits, but by their belief. Listen, people with a strong belief in themselves and their purposes and plans have accomplished extraordinary results. In 1840 experts said, "Anyone traveling at the speed of 30 mph would surely suffocate. In 1878, "Electric lights are unworthy of serious attention" In 1901, "No possible combination can be united into a practical machine by which men shall fly" Then in 1926 "(From a Scientist) "This foolish idea of shooting at the moon is basically impossible" Let me continue... In 1930 (another Scientist) said, "To harness energy locked up in a matter is impossible." There will always be people who say it cannot be done. That is what the "experts" said. The real tragedy is 99% believed them.

I read the 2011 authorized biography of Steve Jobs, by Walter Isaacson and Steve created Apple Computer, was kicked out, and then returned as one of the most incredible leaders of all time. He revolutionized how the entire world experiences computers, applications, music, animation, tablets, and telephones.

Why? Steve had sky-high expectations. He believed impossible things could happen. Steve believed so firmly that obstacles could be overcome that the guys at Apple invented a term called "Steve's reality distortion field." The world has a Reality Discouragement Field. The marketplace of business and finance thinks impossible things are possible. They have raised their expectations, while most people have lowered their exceptions. Expectations matter! Extraordinary people expect more from life, and they almost always get it! You don't receive what you deserve you get what you EXPECT. Faith and believing is Expecting.

Don't ever allow anyone else's limiting beliefs to become yours

My friend Joel Osteen said, "When was the last time you declared "I can" out loud? He said most people tend to magnify their limitations. They focus on their shortcomings." The only limits you have are the limits you believe. Be limitless by believing in the impossible. Start believing impossible things are possible. You gotta believe! The "I Can" is way more important than the IQ. The "I Can" is the sense of possibility dwelling within you, the power and faith within you that gives you strength to do the impossible. It pulls you to express the greatness, the glory, and the wonder to empower you to get up and move forward. Paul said in Philippians 4:13 (NKJV), *"I CAN DO ALL THINGS through Christ who strengthens me."* Listen, if someone tells you "You Can't" he/she is showing you their limits, not yours.

There is Power in Faith and Belief

No one is ready to get up until they believe they can get up! You must believe you can succeed before you do. Napoleon Hill said, "There is a difference between wishing for a thing... and being ready to receive it." Unbending belief and unshakable faith are the essential elements in having the ability to stand up after you have been knocked down. All great achievers and champions have an absolute belief no matter what the circumstances are in their life things can get better. God is not playing favorites, reaching down and touching a select few. The people who succeed and win are those with the strongest faith. Don't ever waste time having faith one minute, and then allowing yourself to sink back into fear and doubt the next. You must believe! Don't stop believing!

"To believe in the things you can see and can touch is no belief at all," Abraham Lincoln said, "but to believe in the unseen is both a triumph and a blessing." Faith and belief act as powerful agents of achievement and success in this life. Believing is the process of receiving and manifesting the reality of hope in one's life. Mark 9:23 (NIV) says, *"If you can believe, all things are possible to him who believes."* Believing is the verb form of faith, it is faith in action, a dominant force just waiting to be used. There is no situation in your life too difficult to turn around. Only believe! You can get what you believe for!

Has the experience of failure and being knocked down sucked the life out of you that you cannot even get back up? In his classic best selling book, The Power of Positive Thinking, Dr. Norman Vincent Peale said this about belief: "Change your mental habits into BELIEF instead of DISBELIEF. In so doing, you bring everything into the realm of possibility." Dr. Peale's empowering message of I CAN is a much better approach then I CAN'T. Scientific research proves that negative beliefs can cause negative circumstanes. Beliefs can be so strong they become self-fulfilling. The famous professional golf legend Arnold Palmer had a plaque in his office that read, "If you think you are beaten, you are. If you think you dare not, you don't. If you'd like to win but think you can't, it's almost certain that you won't. Life's battles don't always go to the stronger woman or man. But sooner or later, those who win are those who think they can."

In the 1920s through 1950s, science and what then passed for sports medicine held that the human body was simply incapable of such unbelievable performance of running a mile in less than four minutes. The "Experts" of that day said that the lungs could not process enough oxygen to sustain the effort; they would burst under strain, as would the heart. They went on to say that the bones would fracture, the joints would rupture and ruin muscles, ligaments, and tendons would tear and fail under much stress and strain. Their belief created a mental barrier. Their conclusion: A human being running a mile in under four minutes was just not possible.

Until May 6th, 1954, in Oxford, England, when a young medical student named Roger Bannister ran a mile in 3 minutes, 59.4 seconds. Bannister believed it was possible and achieved it. With his historic run, he broke not only the physical four-minute barrier but a universal barrier held by "experts." The amazing thing was within another three years another runner duplicated Bannister's feat, and in the years following, hundreds of other runners did it too. Today thousands of runners around the world have run a mile in under four minutes. Why? Roger Bannister proved it was possible by believing it was possible. Belief is so powerful and proves there is no such thing as "impossible."

The Right Source brings the Right Outcome

I love what I John 5:4 (NIV) says, *"For everyone born of God overcomes the world. This is the victory that has overcome the world, even our faith."* The word, Overcomes (Nikos) means, To conquer, Champion of the games. That my friend is extraordinary. The victory to be an overcomer, an achiever, successful, a winner, a champion is already within you. Romans 8:37 (NIV) declares, *"No, in all these things we are more than conquerors through him who loved us."* The word "more than conquerors" is defined as "hypernikos" which means, more than, over above and beyond, greater, top notch, paramount, and overwhelming enormous. The definition describes the kind of faith and belief that is already within you. This is why Jesus said in Mark 9:23 NIV - *'If you can'?" said Jesus. "Everything is possible for one who believes."* Faith tunes us into the divine power that originates from God. Because of that, Jesus clearly said, that you can even do what He did if you believe, and you can do more. Faith and belief turn on the switch to the power that has always been present. The power is not that you "believe in" it is because you "believe upon". On what? The source, which is God. Your faith and belief is the activity that moves you forward, and it helps you get up. Get up every day and tell yourself "I CAN DO THIS!"

Here is some food for thought: Researches and Dartmouth Medical School charted the progress of 232 elderly patients who had undergone open-heart surgery. The researchers discovered that the patients who did not regularly participate in social groups, whether it was a church or social club, were three times more likely to die within six months of their surgery. WOW. In the conclusion of the research one doctor wrote, "Having strong faith and being embedded in a web of relationships like church going have definite health benefits." My conclusion…Doctors should start writing a prescription that says, "Believe in God and go to Church every week." It sounds funny but should be correct. It is possible for people who believe in God and are connected with other people to live a healthier and happier life and be more successful than people who do not.

Having faith and believing is not something you can simply instill within yourself. It must have a source. The source of my faith and belief to achieve and succeed is God. There is an extraordinary result in believing in this source. With feeling, emotion, and beyond a shadow of a doubt, you can believe your life is better. You can achieve greatness, and accomplish your goals, and success on your terms is attainable.

Faith always sees the possibilities. Faith will look past the obstacles. Faith will renew your passion for your dreams that you thought died. Faith will ignite action to move forward and not give up.

Chapter 4

Courage: Defeating Discouragement

Discouragement and failure are two of the surest stepping stones to success.

Dale Carnegie #robberbs

Be on your guard; stand firm in the faith; be courageous; be strong.

I Corinthians 16:13

In spite of everything I shall rise again: I will take up my pencil, which I have forsaken in my great discouragement, and I will go on with my drawing.

Vincent Van Gogh #robberbs

There is a plague sweeping the country today. It is not the Beijing flu, cancer, or even the common cold. This outbreak, however, can be just as deadly as the most dreaded disease known to man, it is called the epidemic of discouragement. We have the world figured out, the wind is at our back, and something goes wrong that deflates us. It is an age-old problem, with an age-old solution.

It is universal. None of us are immune to discouragement. Everyone you have ever known has been discouraged at one time or another. It is recurring. It is highly contagious. Dr. Charles Stanley said, "(Discouragement) Can be temporary–or it can destroy our life. The choice is ours. If we refuse to deal with discouragement head-on, we are opening the door for it to dominate our life completely." During our times of battles, we need the courage to continue strong. Courage is a character trait we need most of all when we face defeat. Without courage, we can lose heart and get discouraged. It is no accident that the word courage means a brave heart, but the word discourage means to lose heart. Discouragement is the result of losing heart in the light of the pressures life presents.

Discouragement is to lose courage or hope; it is to become overwhelmed or lose heart. When we are discouraged, it is easy to want to quit and stop doing the very things in our hearts. Discouragement says, "What is the use of trying anymore? Isn't it time to just give up and make the best of it? To overcome discouragement, we must become courageous. We must take on a stance of courage, tenacity, and bravery. Our most significant test of courage is to refuse to accept discouragement. We only fail when we quit trying. Pressing against an opposing force strengthens us. We grow weak when we do nothing. We need to get up, face the trials in our lives and act. These are the enemies of discouragement. Remembering to turn to God for strength will give us the most courage we can have.

On the front porch of his little country store in Illinois, Abraham Lincoln and Berry, his partner, stood. Business was all gone, and Berry asked, "How much longer can we keep this going?" Lincoln answered, "It looks as if our business has just about winked out." Then he continued, "You know, I wouldn't mind so much if I could just do what I want to do. I want to study law. I wouldn't mind so much if we could sell everything we've got and pay all our bills and have just enough left over to buy one book--Blackstone's Commentary on English Law, but I guess I can't." A strange-looking wagon was coming up the road. The driver angled it up close to the store porch, then looked at Lincoln and said, "I'm trying to move my family out west, and I'm out of money. I've got a good barrel here that I could sell for fifty cents." Abraham Lincoln's eyes went along the wagon and came to the wife looking at him pleadingly, face thin and emaciated. Lincoln ran his hand into his pocket and took out, according to him, "The last fifty cents I had" and said, "I reckon I could use a good barrel."

All day long the barrel sat on the porch of that store. Berry kept chiding Lincoln about it. Late in the evening Lincoln walked out and looked down into the barrel. He saw something in the bottom of it, papers that he had not noticed before. His long arms went down into the barrel, and as Lincoln fumbled around, hit something solid. He pulled out a book and stood petrified: it was Blackstone's Commentary on English Law. Lincoln later wrote, "I stood there holding the book and looking up toward the heavens. There came a deep impression on me that God had something for me to do and He was showing me now that I had to get ready for it. Why this miracle otherwise?" When the world is crashing around you, you do not want to hear God can, and will, use your circumstances to lead you out of the darkness. It is not what you want to hear, but it is what you need to understand.

Courage Counts

Winston Churchill once said, "Success is never final. Failure is never fatal. It is courage that counts". Courage is what makes someone capable of facing extreme danger and/or difficulty without retreating. It implies not only bravery and a dauntless spirit but the ability to endure times of adversity. James Allen said, "You will never do anything worthwhile in this world without courage". Life requires courage.

What is courage? Courage is mastering our fears and getting on with the wonderful things life has to offer — even when it appears when there is no road which to travel. Courage is flourishing in adversity and facing head on life's disappointments. It is not allowing fear to take over and control your life. It is making plans for ways to overcome those fears. Courage is a kind of strength, power or resolves to meet a scary circumstance head-on. Courage is called upon whenever one confronts a difficult, frightening, painful or disturbing situation, when your resources are challenged or pushed to the absolute limit when you feel threatened, weak, vulnerable, intimidated or terrified, and when your first instinctive reaction is to flee. At such times, life is begging an existential question of you: Can you find the courage to face and defeat your fear, or will you be defeated by it? Can you call forth what theologian Paul Tillich called our "courage to be"? Or will you cowardly choose instead, as Shakespeare's Hamlet deliberates, "Not to be?" Courage is synonymous with bravery and fortitude.

You need the courage to encounter fate, defeat despair constructively, and to find and fulfill your destiny heroically. For example, when composer Ludwig van Beethoven discovered he was losing his hearing at the age of twenty-eight, he became understandably depressed about his unfortunate fate. He fell into despair. Then rage. Eventually, his anger gave him the courage needed to encounter his fate and fulfill his musical destiny, resolving to "rise superior to every obstacle" and "take Fate by the throat." Despite total deafness, Beethoven bravely went on to compose his most heroic and beautiful music right up until his death at fifty-seven.

Everyone gets Weak, Afraid, and Discouraged

Courage is not the absence of fear, but moving ahead despite fear. For if there is no fear, who needs courage? Of course, encouragement--the supportive provision of exhortation. Joshua was at a crucial time in his life. He was being coached and mentored by God to make an internal and external transition. To go from following to leading, to step into a new role, a new place, a new position in life. Moses had died, and it was Joshua's time to take his place to lead this nation. He was dealing with some major struggles and insecurities, even though he was a qualified, reliable, and courageous leader.

So God coaches him in Joshua 1:5-9 NIV and says 5 *"No one will be able to stand against you all the days of your life. As I was with Moses, so I will be with you; I will never leave you nor forsake you. 6 Be strong and courageous, because you will lead these people to inherit the land I swore to their ancestors to give them. 7 "Be strong and very courageous. Be careful to obey all the law my servant Moses gave you; do not turn from it to the right or the left, that you may be successful wherever you go. 8 Keep this Book of the Law always on your lips; meditate on it day and night, so that you may be careful to do everything written in it. Then you will be prosperous and successful. 9 Have I not commanded you? Be strong and courageous. Do not be afraid; do not be discouraged, for the Lord your God will be with you wherever you go."*

Why? People will face Discouragement and the feeling of despair in the face of obstacles. It traps you inside yourself. It is subtle in its attack and powerful in its ability to paralyze your progress! I remember John Wayne saying, "Courage is being scared to death but saddling up anyway". Courage is the empowering experience of a decision to stand up and withstand the "slings and arrows of outrageous fortune." And, when wounded or knocked down, to pick oneself up, dust oneself off, and "keep on keepin' on." A choice to stand and fight when appropriate rather than run. To tolerate or attack rather than cower and withdraw. To persevere rather than quit. To act with integrity rather than expedience. To take responsibility rather than slough it off. To embrace reality rather than retreat from it. To move forward in life rather than regress or stagnate. To create rather than destroy. To love rather than hate. To deal with one's demons rather than not.

When you become courageous you are refusing to quit even when you are intimidated by impossibility. It is keeping heart in the face of disappointment, and looking at defeat never as an end but as a fresh start, a new beginning.

If you are faced with discouragement, then it is time to fight, not pout or shrink. You need faith fueled courage. Refuse to let discouragement choke you. An ancient proverb reminds us, "Courage consists not so much in avoiding danger as in conquering it." Like Napoleon Hill, author of the best selling book, "Think and Grow Rich" said, "What we do not see, what most of us never suspect of existing, is the silent but irresistible power which comes to the rescue of those who fight on in the face of discouragement."

Chapter 5

Perseverance...It's Always Too Soon To Quit

"I hated every minute of training, but I said Don't quit, suffer now and live the rest of your life like a champion"

Mohammad Ali

Blessed is the one who perseveres under trial because, having stood the test, that person will receive the crown of life that the Lord has promised to those who love him.

James 1:12 NIV

"By perseverance the snail reached the ark

Charles Spurgeon

In 1972, NASA launched the exploratory space probe Pioneer 10. The satellite's primary mission was to reach Jupiter, photograph it and its moons, and beam data it collected about this giant planet back to earth. Scientists regarded this as a bold plan, because up until then no satellites had gone beyond Mars, and they feared the asteroid belt would destroy the satellite before it would ever get to Jupiter. But Pioneer 10 accomplished its mission and much, much more. Flying past

Jupiter in November 1973, the space probe continued its incredible journey toward the edge of our solar system. At one billion miles from the sun, Pioneer 10 passed Saturn. At some two billion miles, it hurtled past the planet Uranus, then past Neptune, at nearly three billion miles, and Pluto, at almost four billion miles.

By 1997, 25 years after its launch, Pioneer 10 was more than six billion miles from the sun. And it's still going. Though now nearly 8 billion miles from the sun, the satellite keeps sending signals; some were received as recently as April 27, 2002. And despite the immense distance, Pioneer 10 continues to beam back radio signals to scientists on Earth. Commenting on the Pioneer 10 in Time magazine Leon Jaroff says, "Perhaps most remarkable, is the fact that those signals emanate from an eight-watt transmitter, which radiates about as much power as a bedroom night-light, and takes more than nine hours to reach Earth." "The Little Satellite That Could" was not qualified to do what it did. Engineers designed Pioneer 10 with a useful life of only three years. But it has kept going and going and going. By simple longevity, its small eight-watt transmitter radio accomplished more than anyone thought possible.

So it is when we offer ourselves to serve the Lord. God can work even through someone with only eight-watt abilities. God cannot work, however, through someone who gives up and quits. Do not be discouraged if your plans do not succeed the first time. No one learns to walk by taking only one step.

Are you thinking about quitting? Join the club. Everyone thinks about quitting something sometimes. There is a big difference between quitting and wanting to quit. How many times do we become discouraged, impatient and ready to throw in the towel? (This an old saying that comes from the world of Boxing. When one of the boxers has gone as far as he can go, his manager throws a towel into the ring to signal that the match is forfeited). One of my favorite movie series is Rocky. I was thinking while watching it with my sons, why is it that people love Rocky so much. Was it for his accent? His intelligence? No, it was because of his heart. When Rocky would fight, it did not matter how many times he got knocked down; Rocky always got back up. He did not quit. He persevered. You know, the people who I have come to respect over the years are not the flashy or even the most gifted people, but it is the people who never quit. Those who hang in there and never give up. Like Rocky Balboa, they get knocked down, but they never stay down, they are always back up on their feet, rearing' to go. The reality in life is you will get knocked down. It happens to even the best. But you must never give up! Jay Z once said, "The genius thing that we did was, We didn't give up.

Falling does not make you a failure, but staying down does! Do not Quit!

Great works are performed not by strength but by perseverance. The word "perseverance" is defined as steadfastness in doing something despite difficulty, discouragement, or delay in achieving success. Extraordinary and successful people have three dominant traits. 1. They Respond positively to all challenges and learn from mistakes 2. Take personal initiative and 3. They have great perseverance. Those who persevere are always the ones left standing when everyone else quits. We should never give in and never give up. Never, never, never, never-in nothing, great or small, large or petty--never give up! Never yield to the overwhelming might of the enemy.

I have given up before. I know the results of failure and success. I know how it feels when a dream dies. I have pastored churches for 23 years in Ohio and Tennessee. But I had a dream to plant a church in Columbus, Ohio. My family and I launched and planted GraceTown Church in 2011 with the help of my network and tribe, The Association of Related Churches. Throughout the first four years, we experienced success, growth, and influence. Many people were connecting, attending, and growing during that time. Then we began to have trouble. Because of dream killers, toxic people and some not so right decisions, we suffered from many people leaving and the church struggling. I had to make the difficult decision of shutting down the weekend services. That was one of the most difficult decisions I had to make. Internally, over the past two years I have been in the most challenging fight of my life, personally, financially, organizationally, emotionally, spiritually, and with our family. I know what it is like to be knocked down hard.

Jeff Bezos, Amazon Founder and CEO said, "I knew that if I failed I wouldn't regret that, but I knew the one thing I might regret is not trying." I do not regret moving my family to Columbus; I do not regret starting the church, I do not regret pouring thousands of dollars of my finances into the organization, I do not regret the hours I gave people, because I know it made a difference in lives and many were changed. I do know that I have a resolution on the inside of me to keep going, keep loving, keep forgiving, keep writing, keep speaking, and keep inspiring people.

It took Winston Churchill three years to get through the eighth grade because he had trouble learning English. In kind of an ironic twist, years later in the midst of World War II Oxford University asked then Prime Minister Churchill to address its commencement exercises. Dressed in his finest suit, he arrived at the auditorium where the service was to be held with his usual props, a cigar, a cane and a top hat. As Churchill approached the podium, the crowd rose in appreciative applause. Standing there looking very dignified, he settled the crowd down and asked them to be seated. Standing confidently before this crowd of great admirers, he removed his cigar and placed his top hat on the podium. Then Churchill gazed at his waiting audience that included some of the most noted scholars in the world. With an authoritative tone in his voice, he began with three words: "Never give up!" Several seconds passed without him saying another word. Finally, he repeated those same three words, "Never give up!" There was a deafening silence as Churchill reached for his hat and cigar, steadied himself with his cane and left the platform. He finished his commencement address.

Develop a form of resiliency where even when life deals you a blow

Many years ago, during a Monday night football game between the Chicago Bears and the New York Giants, one of the announcers observed that Walter Payton, the Bears' running back, had accumulated over nine miles in career rushing yardage. The other announcer remarked, "Yeah, and that's with someone knocking him down every 4.6 yards!" Even the best get knocked down, but what makes them the best is they get back up. The key to success is to get up and run again just as hard. The key is to be persistent and never give up no matter how hard you get hit.

When you get knocked down, do not stay down, always get back up. Develop a form of resiliency, so when life deals you a blow, you get back up charging. There was a page from John Wesley's Diary reads as follows: Sunday morning, May 5, preached in St. Ann's, was asked not to come back anymore. Sunday p.m., May 5, preached at St. John's, deacons said, "Get out and stay out." Sunday a.m., May 12, preached at St. Jude's, can't go back there either. Sunday p.m., May 12, preached at St. George's, kicked out again. Sunday a.m., May 19, preached at St. somebody else's, deacons called special meeting and said I couldn't return. Sunday p.m., May 19, preached on the street, kicked off the street. Sunday a.m., May 26, preached in a meadow, chased out of meadow as a bull was turned loose during the services. Sunday a.m., June 2, preached out at the edge of town, kicked off the highway. Sunday p.m., June 2, afternoon service, preached in a pasture, 10,000 people came to hear me. Don't give up.

Look what the writer in Psalm 18:31-37 NIV said, *"For who is God besides the Lord? And who is the Rock except for our God? 32 It is God who arms me with strength and keeps my way secure. 33 He makes my feet like the feet of a deer; he causes me to stand on the heights. 34 He trains my hands for battle; my arms can bend a bow of bronze. 35 You make your saving help my shield, and your right hand sustains me; your help has made me great. 36 You provide a broad path for my feet so that my ankles do not give way. 37 I pursued my enemies and overtook them; I did not turn back till they were destroyed."*

In 1933, Charles Darrow brought "Monopoly" to the Parker Brothers Company. The experts of the company rejected the game citing 52 fundamental errors. After the rejection, Mr. Darrow spent a year and persevered, and in 1936 Parker Brothers agreed to sell the game, and Charles Darrow became a multi-millionaire. Since that time, over 275 million copies of Monopoly have been sold in 111 countries and 43 languages. Today, with 485 million players around the globe, Monopoly is the most commercially successful board game in the world. All because Mr. Darrow persevered and never gave up. Henry Wadsworth Longfellow once said,

"Perseverance is a great element of success. If you only knock long enough and loud enough at the gate, you are sure to wake somebody up."

Here are the facts, God empowers, fuels, and assists those who have the heart to keep on going and not give up. There is something to be said of someone who perseveres. Think about this; Perseverance is rooted in "Severe" which means, great discomfort, damage, dangerous, distress, difficult. Stretch or extreme. No one needs to persevere when everything is good and easy. No, one needs to persevere when it is the most difficult. It reminds me of the story of the Two frogs that fell into a deep cream bowl. One was an optimistic soul. But the other took the gloomy view. "We'll drown," he lamented without much ado, and with a last despairing cry, he flung up his legs and said "Goodbye." Quote the other frog with a steadfast grin, "I can't get out, but I won't give in, I'll just swim around till my strength is spent, then I'll die the more content." Bravely he swam to work his scheme, and his struggles began to churn the cream. The more he swam, his legs a flutter, the more the cream turned into butter. On top of the butter at last he stopped, and out of the bowl, he gaily hopped.

What is the moral? It is easily found. If you cannot hop out, keep swimming around! The key to winning and success merely is never quit until you have won. The seed of greatness lies within you.

Prayer the Empowering Key To Perseverance

One of the most powerful keys in persevering is developing a discipline and habit of prayer. Prayer is the most difficult thing in the world to do. In prayer we find ourselves standing on the edge of a deep, dark, abyss, the world of the divine, infinite, and eternal. We come face to face with ourselves and face to face with God. Prayer is seeking to weave the God's will and purpose into your life, relationships, your worries, your fears and failures and into your broken and fallen world.

Prayer is about conversing with God, but it is also about collaborating with His actions in the world. You will not experience the renewal and strength you seek until you ask God to send his Holy Spirit to change your heart and your life.

Developing a consistent time everyday day to pray will strengthen your inner life. Which is an important part of your relationship with God? Yet, too often you neglect this communication with your heavenly Father.

In many cases, you don't pray because you don't know exactly how to pray, or how often, or what to say. One is so busy with a million pursuits that he/she does not even notice the most important things slipping away. You are overwhelmed by the pace of life - 24/7 nonstop — it's the mantra of your culture. You live in an agitated, uptight and fast-paced world filled with stress. You are frazzled, overwhelmed, complexed, & bewildered. You have heavier workloads, greater demands, higher stress than ever before, and you are busy busy busy.

If you do not break the tensions of daily living, they will break you!

"I just don't have the time" is the excuse we hear so often. Every person has the same amount of time each week - 168 hours. You make time for things that are important. Too often you give God only the tired remnants of your time. You do not have time for everything — you must make time for things that count. It is not a matter of time; it is a matter of priorities. Andy Stanley said, "We don't drift in good directions. We discipline and prioritize ourselves there." Prayer should be our first language, not a foreign language. It should be our first response, not our last resort.

The great soccer player, Michelle Akers said it was prayer that assisted in her outstanding soccer performance. She said the summer during the World Cup I was battling chronic fatigue syndrome. It is an illness she has been fighting with for years. Often feeling overwhelmed and weary during the soccer matches and even training sessions. During those times of feeling so bad, I was so tempted to quit. So out on the fields during the World Cup, I kept quoting out loud my favorite Bible Verse, Joshua 1:9 (paraphrased), " I've commanded you to be strong and brave. Don't ever be afraid or discouraged! She prayed those words game after game, time after time, practice after practice and said it was what got her through. Prayer is what is powerful and prayer is what will work when everything else does not.

In Luke 18:1 NIV it says, *"Then Jesus told his disciples a parable to show them that they should always pray and not give up."* The word "Should" is also the word (Ought in the King James Version) and it means we are under obligation, we are bound, and it is necessary for us to pray always. CS Lewis said, "I pray because I can't help myself. I pray because I'm helpless. I pray because the need flows out of me all the time — waking and sleeping. It doesn't change God - It changes me."

We need to recover this ancient Christian practice and reignite the fire of prayer in our hearts! I've learned over the past two years the secret to my peace and power in the midst of great stress, discouragement, disappointments, and frustrations of everyday life, business, and family is that I have a divine connection with God through learning to pray and meditate on a daily basis. Even in the midst of great stress, I wanted to give up, but there was a tenacity on the inside of me that kept telling me to not give up.

Several years ago Charles Stanley said that he was struggling with some opposition. During that time an elderly woman from his church invited him to her retirement community for lunch. Although he was very busy and under some serious pressure, he went and ate lunch with her. Afterwards she took him up to her apartment and showed him a picture hanging on her living room wall. It was a picture of Daniel in the lion's den. She said, "Young man, look at this picture and tell me what you see." Dr. Stanley looked at the picture and saw that all the lions had their mouths closed, some were lying down. Daniel was standing with his hands behind him. Stanley told the lady everything he knew to tell her. Then she asked, "Anything else?" He knew there must be, but he couldn't see anything else. She put her arm on his shoulder and said, "What I want you to see is that Daniel doesn't have his eyes on the lions, he has his eyes on the Lord."

The Primary purpose of prayer is not to get God to do what we think God ought to do but to be properly formed spiritually. We are not called to manage or advise God. Prayer puts our eyes on God! Prayer must be a necessity, not an option! Not only is it a privilege but it's a duty! It's a blessing not boring! When we develop a habit a of prayer and meditation it keeps us from fainting and giving up. Fainting here is not a physical problem of a temporary loss of consciousness as a result of inadequate blood to the brain. Fainting is a spiritual and mental condition posing a constant danger to all individuals unless they pray! Faint defined is to be weak, to fail in heart, to be weary. To toil, to tire, to be sickened. Prayer keeps us from fainting. We live in a time where we are dealing with pressures, weariness, strife, problems, financial difficulties, oppression. It's enough to make even the strongest of people weary.

Paul encourages everyone in Galatians 6:9 NIV - *"Let us not become weary in doing good, for at the proper time we will reap a harvest if we do not give up."* Why? Prayer is one of the most rejuvenating, reviving, restful, experiences a person can be engaged in. Not so much for the body, because prayer is work, it is action, it is movement. But for the mind, soul, spirit, and heart of a person, a prayerful life is a powerful life! A prayerless life is a powerless life! Dwight Moody once said, " When a man has no strength, if he leans on God, he becomes powerful."

God Makes extravagant promises about what He does WHEN WE PRAY. So do not give up, do not get frustrated, disappointed, or lose hope. Praying is what we do in our time, and the answer happens in God's time. I would encourage you to find a quiet place and a calm and tranquil state of mind. Take a few deep breaths and make sure you are comfortable. Sit quietly and in silence and invite the Holy Spirit to guide your prayers. One prayer can change ANYTHING. One prayer can change EVERYTHING. Let me remind you again: Do not give up! Do not back down! Tenacious unsinkable people do not quit because of circumstances, rejections, or problems! They persevere!

Chapter 6

Master The Small Things To Make a Big Difference

"It's the little things that are vital. Little things make big things happen."

John Wooden—UCLA: Won 10 NCAA championships #robberbs

Whatever the mind of a man can conceive and believe, it can achieve. Thoughts are things! Strong, deeply rooted desire is the starting point for all achievement.

Napoleon Hill #robberbs

If you change the way you look at things, the things you look at change."

Wayne Dyer #robberbs

In 1942, the New York Yankees and the Washington Senators played in the World Series. It was a very close series. At the end of six games, it was tied at three games. The stadium was filled for the deciding game, played in Washington. They came to the ninth inning with the score tied at two. New York was put down in order, and Washington came to bat. The home team screamed for one lone run which would win the series and the World Championship. The first two men made outs and it looked like extra innings. Then a player named Goslin came to the plate. Two strikes were called and then two balls. The crowd was watching every pitch. On the fifth pitch, Goslin stepped into the ball and slammed it to left center field. The crowd became delirious; it looked like a home run, but it hit six inches below the top of the wall and fell back into the playing field. Goslin was slowing down for a triple when the third base coach signaled him to try for an infield home run. He ran for home. The shortstop took the peg from left center, spinning to fire the ball to the catcher. Goslin slid into home in a cloud of dust, seemingly a split second before the tag. The umpire made a delayed call, and finally, as the dust cleared, he raised his right-hand shouting, "You're out!" The Washington fans were furious. Washington managers and players rushed out to argue the call. The umpire announced he would consult with the other umpires. After the four umpires conferred for a minute or two the umpire announced: "Ladies and gentlemen, the batter is out because he did not touch first base!"

The mistake was so simple; the runner missed first base, so he was out. It is elementary in the game of baseball. You have to touch the bases. It is the same thing in life and business. The simple little things are what needs to be mastered. It is often the small things that no one sees that results in the big things that everyone wants. Small things like our thoughts and our words.

You Will Never Change Your Life Until You Change the Way You Think

James Allen in his best selling book, "As A Man Thinketh" said, "You are today where your thoughts have brought you; you will be tomorrow where your thoughts take you." Your thoughts are like trains they will take you somewhere. Therefore, life will always move in the direction of your strongest thoughts. Solomon even said in Proverbs 23:7 (NKJV) *"For as he thinks in his heart, so is he..."* In other words, You are not what you think you are, but what you think, you are.

Henry Ford said, "If you think you can, you're right. If you think you can't, you're right." Why? Because your mind is the drawing room for your tomorrow. What happens in your mind will happen in time. Benjamin Disraeli said, "Nurture your mind with great thoughts, for you will never go any higher than you think." Nothing limits extraordinary achievement like small thinking; Nothing expands possibilities like unleashed extraordinary thinking. Earl Nightingale, Founder of the Nightingale-Conant Company, said, " The secret to success is simple, you become what you think about." You may agree or disagree, but the truth is that your thoughts are powerful.

There is nothing more powerful than a changed mind! You can change your hair color. Your address. Your residence. Your clothes. But if you do not change your thinking, the same experiences in your life will perpetually happen over and over. If you want things to be extraordinary on the outside, you HAVE to have extraordinary thinking on the inside! Mark Twain said, "Take your mind out every now and then and dance on it. It is getting all caked up."

Your future does not respond to anyone's thoughts but your OWN!

Your life will always move in the direction of your strongest thoughts. Proverbs 4:23 NCV *"Be careful what you think because your thoughts run your life."* Mike Murdock said, "God gave us two primary functions of our mind, memory and imagination." "Our memories replay our past." "Our imagination preplays our future." Your thoughts and words trigger images. Your imagination is not evil; it is a gift from God. Why? We think in pictures. Where is your mind taking you? Albert Einstein said, "Logic will take you from A to B, but imagination will take you everywhere!"

In your mind, you can look back at your past or look forward to your future. You decide. Your mind is not restricted by location. God gave you a MIND so He can give you a picture of where He wants to take you. God paints your future success, significance, peace, prosperity, and joys on the canvas of your mind. The best time to start improving your tomorrow is always now. Why wait? The thoughts you think today determines what happens tomorrow! Make sure you are thinking right thoughts every day.

Unlock the Power of Possibility Thinking

Your mind is the drawing room for your tomorrow. What happens in your mind will happen in time. Dr. Robert Schuller quoted, wrote, and preached on the power of possibility thinking. He said, "It takes but one positive thought when given a chance to survive and thrive to overpower an entire army of negative thoughts." Stop focusing on the impossibilities. Take the word out of your vocabulary. Do not reduce God down to the size of your brain. We need to think with a mind of faith and possibilities. Otherwise, you will limit yourself. In Mark 10:27 Jesus looked at people and said to them, *"With man, this is impossible, but not with God; all things are possible with God."* Did you see that? All things are possible. Audrey Hepburn said, "Nothing is impossible. The word itself says I'm Possible!"

I used to weigh around 230 pounds. I was a 38-40 waist, XL shirt, Size 46 suit, etc....I knew that if I was going to lose weight I had to change my mindset about eating, exercising, and my health. I started to think differently and speak different contrary to how I looked. Things began to shift, but sometimes things can get worse before they get better. In 2008 I was diagnosed with Type 2 Diabetes, and that changed everything. I had no other choice but to change my outside but it started with my thinking. I began disciplined eating habits, and the process began. I am not always perfect today with my eating habits. Today my weight is 150 pounds; I wear a 30 waist pant, medium shirt, and size 38 suit. I am still working to heal myself of Type 2 Diabetes. If changes are to be made in one's life, you have to think different and think positive no matter what the circumstance is to make those changes.

Possibility and positive mindsets produce positive lives. Negative minds will always produce negative lives. Take charge of the way you look at every day and every situation. There is a lot in life you cannot change. But you can change your thinking. The positive possibility thinker sees the opportunity in every difficulty!

Isaiah 55:9 says *"As the heavens are higher than the earth, so are my ways higher than your ways and my thoughts than your thoughts."* Simply stated that God's thoughts are pretty high. Higher than ours. Amos 4:13 NIV says *"He who forms the mountains, who creates the wind, and who reveals his thoughts to mankind, who turns dawn to darkness, and treads on the heights of the earth— the Lord God Almighty is his name."* Isn't that awesome? The God who set the mountains in place puts the thoughts in your mind. How you think matters to God! God not only wants to help you control your thoughts. But He wants to take your thoughts higher, to the next level.

You will never change the way you think until you change the way you talk.

Solomon, who was the wisest man who ever lived, besides Jesus, said in Proverbs 18:21 NIV *"The tongue has the power of life and death, and those who love it will eat its fruit."* Words have extraordinary power. Words were an important element in God's work of creation. The plan of creation had been set in place, but God had to speak the words before it could become a visible reality. Words carry creative power!

The difference between the right word and the almost right word is the difference between lightning and a lightning bug — Mark Twain

The Words you speak indicate what you believe in your heart and ultimately determine what you will receive in life. Start saying things you want to happen in your life, not what you do not want to happen! Remember, Every time you open your mouth, your mind walks out and parades up and down the words.

Jesus said in Luke 6:45 NIV - *"A good man brings good things out of the good stored up in his heart, and an evil man brings evil things out of the evil stored up in his heart." "For the mouth speaks what the heart is full of."* Which means anyone who controls their words is protecting their own life. Look at what Proverbs 13:2-3 NLT says- *"Wise words will win you a good meal, but treacherous people have an appetite for violence."* Those who control their tongue will have a long life; opening your mouth can ruin everything. You decide if you want lips of life or tongues of trouble! If you ever realize how powerful your mind and your mouth are, you will never give space to another negative thought or word. I love to fish, and I have never seen a fish on the wall with its mouth closed. It is always open.

Another scripture is in Matthew 12:34-37 The Message - *"You have minds like a snake pit! How do you suppose what you say is worth anything when you are so foul-minded? It is your heart, not the dictionary, that gives meaning to your words. A good person produces good deeds and words season after season. An evil person is a blight on the orchard. Let me tell you something: Every one of these careless words is going to come back to haunt you. There will be a time of Reckoning."* Words are powerful; take them seriously. Words can be your salvation. Words can also be your damnation. If you want to change the life you have, you must change the words you speak. Small changes in the words we speak will make a big difference in the life we live.

Your future does not respond to anyone's voice but your own

My words have the power to set the direction for my life. James made it very clear in James 3:3-5 NLT *"We can make a large horse go wherever we want using a small bit in its mouth. 4 And a small rudder makes a huge ship turn wherever the pilot chooses to go, even though the winds are strong. 5 In the same way, the tongue is a small thing that makes grand speeches. But a tiny spark can set a great forest on fire."* The bit puts pressure on the horse's tongue. Your words are powerful enough to give direction to your entire life. It turns the ship of your life, circumstances, your relationships, and even your businesses.

"Words are the guides to acts; the mouth makes the first move" Rabbi Leon De Modena

Start saying things you want to happen in your life, not what you do not want to happen! Jesus said to speak to the mountain, not about the mountain. Jesus said you could have what you say, but you have been saying what you have. Mark 11:23 ESV *"Truly, I say to you, whoever says to this mountain, 'Be taken up and thrown into the sea,' and does not doubt in his heart, but believes that what he says will come to pass, it will be done for him."* You are not missing it in your believing; you are missing it with your words. The words you speak indicate what you believe in your hearts and ultimately determine what you will receive in life. Your mountains need to hear your voice!

Most people do not understand the connection between the mouth and the mind. They work hand in hand. Two small things that make a big difference. There is a connection between what you are thinking and what you say because you can not separate them. You can not have a thinking message without a words message. At weddings, the minister will say, "Repeat after me," "recite these vows." When a political figure is being sworn into office, or you have to testify in court. You have to say something. Your words matter. Words have power because they create your world.

In 1962, Thomas Kuhn wrote The Structure of Scientific Revolution, and fathered, defined, and popularized the concept of "paradigm shift." Kuhn argued that scientific advancement is not evolutionary, but rather is a "series of peaceful interludes punctuated by intellectually violent revolutions," and in those revolutions, one conceptual world view is replaced by another. He encouraged us to think of a paradigm shift as a change from one way of thinking to another. It is a revolution, a transformation — a metamorphosis.

You will never change the way you think until you change the way you talk. Your mind affects your words and ultimately your actions. Your mouth is the expression of your thoughts.

What you are thinking is expressed in what you say and do. If you change your thinking, you will change your words. If you change your words, then you can reset your future and change your life. A transformed or renewed mind will reset the life that is before you.

There is Power in Affirmations

Jack Canfield, Author of The Success Principles and The Chicken Soup for the Soul series, said, Every thought you think, and every word you say is an affirmation. In scriptures, they are called "confessions." Every day you will be bombarded with all types of negative messages. These messages will come across through the media, social media outlets, coworkers, and even family members. What you do not realize is that these messages end up turning into your beliefs which either propel you to succeed or fail.

I am going to share with you just some of the affirmations that I declare every morning. I believe they have assisted me in moving through difficult days. Remember your words have power. They replaced my negative beliefs, limited ideas, depressing thoughts, and shifted difficult situations in my life. Just start the day by repeating these statements. Do not look for immediate results but say them out loud and with faith. Make it a daily habit. You will eventually make these thoughts and affirmations an actual reality. Keep in mind to make your statements useful in maintaining complete positivity with what you want to do and the person you want to be.

Soren Kierkegaard said, *"Our life always expresses the result of our dominant thoughts."* If that is the case, let your thoughts and your words be positive, prosperous, blessed, and extraordinary.

- I plan for an extraordinary day. My anticipation attracts positive experiences to me.
- I am centered and focused I am at ease.
- The past is over, so it has no power now. The thoughts of this moment create my future.
- I am lovingly supporting my family and helping them to achieve success, wealth, peace, and happiness.
- I am successful in all of my endeavors. Success is my natural state.
- I quickly find solutions to challenges and roadblocks and move past them quickly.
- Mistakes and setbacks are stepping stones to my success because I learn from them.
- Every cell in my body is alive with health and energy.
- I meditate daily to give my body deep rest and enhance my immune system.
- I breathe deeply, bringing energy to all my cells.
- I am moving from poverty thinking to prosperity thinking, and my finances reflect this change.
- God is my infinite supply, and large sums of money come to me quickly and efficiently under the grace of God for the highest good of all concerned. I am now earning...$
- I welcome an unlimited source of income and wealth in my life.
- I use money to better my life and the lives of others.
- I am out of debt; my needs are met, I have plenty more to put in the store.

For more of my affirmations, you can download my free ebook at www.robyanok.com

Chapter 7

Who's in Your Corner?

"He that won't be counseled can't be helped."
Benjamin Franklin #robberbs

"Coaching is preventing mistakes before it happens."
Lou Holtz #robberbs

"With the right people in your corner, you can become unstoppable."
#robberbs

In the boxing movie Million Dollar Baby, Clint Eastwood's new female boxing project named Maggie, played by Hillary Swank, ends up having to face her first opponent with some unknown business man/fight promoter as her manager. Frankie Dunn, Clint's character, is hard-nosed and only promised Maggie that he would train her and not go any further.

This first fight exposes a few of Maggie's weaknesses, while Frankie sits in the stands frustrated with some of her fighting mistakes. In her corner is her "manager" who of course is only interested in making some cash off the fight, not very much concerned about his fighter. Not being able to take any more torture, Frankie leaves the stands and ends up on the side of the ring coaching Maggie with swiftness. In those few minutes Frankie decides to take on the role of manager, and by the next round Maggie takes out her opponent.

Maggie would not have been able to win that first fight, or many after that if she did not have good people in her corner coaching and guiding her. It made all the difference in the world to have Frankie step in and tell her exactly what she needed to do. Having a corner full of good people is essential to every one of us. There is no reason for any of us to go through life's challenges without the help of friends, family, and people that genuinely care about us.

With this said, I ask you this question: Who is in your corner? Who do you have speaking into your life and offering counsel on a daily basis? Who do you entrust with the critical and most valuable parts of your life? Are they giving good counsel? Solid counsel? Unbiased counsel? Who is coaching you? Do they have your best interests in mind or do they merely tell you what you want to hear? When you are watching a boxing match, in between rounds you always see "the corner man" giving the boxer instructions. He is telling him either to stick and move, throw more lefts, go to the body, etc. The corner man is the most important person the boxer has because he can see everything that goes on in the fight. It is all up to the boxer to follow instructions. Not all corner man gives the right instructions, that is why you see boxers constantly changing their corner man. The Cornerman is also the person that tells the boxer not what he wants to hear, but what he NEEDS to hear.

For instance, The fight between "Sugar" Ray Leonard and Thomas"The Hit Man" Hearns. Both were champions in that division; they were fighting to unify the title. It was a great fight, but Hearns looked like he was taking it over. Then in Leonard's corner, you hear Angelo Dundee (Leonard's corner man) telling him " You're blowing it, kid!", You're blowing it, kid." Leonard when out there the next round, and TKO'd Hearns.

The next fight Leonard had was against Roberto Duran. Now Duran is a much harder puncher then Hearns. Angelo Dundee kept telling Leonard don't stand toe to toe with him. But Leonard didn't listen, and what happened? "Sugar" Ray Leonard lost his first fight.

In the rematch against Duran, Leonard did listen. Guess what? He won! All the great champions have a good corner man or woman. That is what separates the winners and the losers. The same goes for people building a business. Whether it be in life, relationships, the marketplace, or business. You have to have someone "in your corner" telling you want you NEED to hear, not what you want to hear. Someone that will be with you through ups and downs. Someone that will encourage you and help you bring out the greatness within you. Don't just listen to anybody! Listen to the people that are successful and are where you want to be! Surround yourself with as many of these people, and you will have the success that you deserve!

You Must Be Coachable

Everybody fights better with good people in their corner. All champions have coaches. People who are willing to wipe the sweat out of your eyes, bandage up your cuts, encourage you and send you back into the fight. You need those people if you ever attempt to do anything at all with your life. I am not even talking yet about living a life of significance. I am talking about just doing anything at all. Life is tough. Do not try to go it alone. Everybody needs a coach to be in their corner. A coach focuses on future possibilities, not past mistakes.

To be coachable is to be trained or tutored, give hints to, prime with facts, and able to receive instruction. It means teachable. The writer in Proverbs 1:5 said, "A wise man will hear and increase in learning. And a man of understanding will attain wise counsel." We have to be open to receive instruction from those in our corner. Don't be a know it all. Be a learn it all. It is not the big changes that move you from good to great but the small subtle changes and adjustments. Being coachable means, you are willing to listen to, take advice from, and learn from those who have more experience than you do.

You Must Learn to Listen

Early in his career, Tiger Woods Golf Coach told him to change his grip and swing if he wanted to continue to win. If Tiger Woods still needs coaching, so do you and I. Why? Because God requires us to be the best that we can be. No one ever wins alone. Andrew Carnegie said, "It marks a big step in your development when you come to realize that other people can help you do a better job than you could do alone."

Many times the best advice is the hardest to hear. Coaches are not committed to our comfort but are committed to our success. They are a prophetic picture of your future. A Coach is not someone who gives you advice, but it is the advice you follow. John Wooden said, "A good coach can change a game, a great coach can change a life." In the movie Creed, an older

Rocky Balboa makes the young fighter Adonis look in the mirror and says to him, "You see this guy here? That is the toughest opponent you are ever going to have to face. I believe that is true in the ring, and I think that is true in life." Most of the time our problem is the person we look at in the mirror. A coach helps us see that. They see more talent and ability within ourselves than we see within ourselves, and they help bring that out of us.

Being coachable means learning to listen. Benjamin Franklin once said, "He that won't be counseled can't be helped." Listening is apart of your recovery, restoration, and success. Numerous times in the scriptures it would say, "He that has an ear let him hear." If you do not listen, you cannot learn. Your ability to listen is the most critical part of your success. Only about 10% of people listen properly, according to several psychological studies. In fact, most people do not know how to listen intelligently, systematically and purposefully. Progress is difficult when you will not listen.

You Must have the Right Coach

The right coach makes the difference. Studies have shown that having the right coach or mentor can make all the difference in your game. Seek them out. Who is your right coach? Teams in the NCAA, NFL, NBA, and MLB spend millions of dollars on getting the right coach for their teams. They are constantly firing, searching, and hiring the best coach.

There are only three kinds of coaches you want in your corner: honest, experienced, and encouraging. If you are going to permit people to speak into your life and give you coaching you want people that are always going to shoot straight with you and not hold back. Of course, you want people to tell you what you would like to hear, but that does you no good. That type of counsel might make you feel good for a little bit, but it is temporary.

I have several people that know they have permission to be very blunt and honest with me. They know that they do not have to take my feelings into account and that I want them to be 100% honest with me. Being straight with a friend or family member and not holding anything back is merely love, and it is only "tough" because most of the time it is not what you want to hear. Trust me; there have been many times in my life where those individuals was that way with me. It may have hurt my feelings, but it healed my life.

So evaluate your coaches and counselors, and your "support systems". Make sure you know they love you and they are honest with you. If the coaching they give you does not make you uncomfortable or challenge you, then maybe they are not being direct with you. I am not talking about people who tear you down or attack you. I am talking about the people who believe in you, who desire to build you and benefit you. And if you had people in your life that did shoot straight and you removed yourself from them because you didn't like what you were hearing, bring those people back in. Reconnect with them. You need them more than you know.

You want people that know what they are talking about. Individuals who have wisdom, experience, and knowledge. Maggie, the boxer, had an experienced fighter in her corner who taught her everything she needed to know. All he had to do during a fight was be there in the corner with her, occasionally reminding her of what she had already been taught.

If you've fallen, made mistakes, or failed, If you're struggling with something or going through a crisis, why have someone in your corner who's worse off than you? Yes, its good to have people to lean on who have been there or are going through the same thing, but they shouldn't be the only ones in your corner. Allow older, wiser people to stand by you. People that may have been there in the past but succeeded at some point and learned from their mistakes. That is wisdom. People that are full of wisdom and strength that can lead and direct you. Allow people that will not only hold you by the hand while you go through all your crap but those that will do some hard work and stand behind you and push you from behind to help you get up the mountain.

Be sure that your corner includes experience that resulted in successful results, not just someone or others that went through something similar, yet never really learned from it. I am sure we can all agree that this life is not easy and will come with daily challenges. I am thankful for the people in my life that are always there ready to not only to hold my hand but also slap me in the back of the head when I do not see things clearly. Take a step back today, wipe your lenses, and make an effort to see more clearly. Make whatever changes you need to make today so that you fill up your corner with good, stable, honest, and experienced people.

There is entirely no reason you should not have a success coach. We all need someone who will help you stay on track and provide us with the fine-tuning that will help us realize our vision for an extraordinary life. Mark Twain, said it best, "Keep away from people who try to belittle your ambitions. Small people always do that, but the great make you feel that you, too, can become great." I can help you! My coaching network, Motivations for Monday Coaching, can help take you to the next level of your life, relationships, business, and career. Email me at rob@robyanok.com or go to www.roby-anok.com

You Must Be Connected

Who are you connected to? Who is your ride or die friend? Relationships are of the utmost importance in life and business. Anthony Robbins said, "Remember; We become who we spend time with. The quality of a person's life is most often a direct reflection of the expectations of their peer group. Choose your friends well." If you see a turtle on the top of a fencepost, you know he had help getting there! There is no such thing as a self-made man or woman. Everything in life, good or bad, has happened because of who we are connected too. We are made for relationships.

It was a tragedy etched in the walls of our memory. Cassie Bernal, with a gun to her head, would not deny her faith in God even though it meant the loss of her life. In the aftermath of the shooting, her parents would tell how Cassie had not always been a committed Christian. In fact, they told how she, herself, had once been a troubled teen participating in a party-lifestyle, writing letters of hatred and anger towards her parents & society. But a remarkable change had occurred in Cassie's life when she began hanging out with a different crowd. Her view of life had radically changed and she became a committed Christian.

When the right people enter your life, the right things happen. Right people are those who will build you and not tear you down. They are excited about your potential and dreams. Laugh when you laugh. Cry when you cry. Make it a priority to strengthen that kind of relationships. Proverbs 13:20 NIV says, *"Walk with the wise and become wise, for a companion of fools suffers harm."* Dr. Carl Menger said, Our environment shapes us more than our DNA or heredity. I Corinthians 15:33 NIV says, "Do not be misled: *"Bad company corrupts good character."* Birds of a feather do walk together.

Relationships will either propel you or sustain you. People are like elevators they take you up or bring you down. So wrong relationships are thieves to your success. Disconnect from the people who take you down and not up, they make withdrawals but never deposits. They abuse and misuse you. They gossip about you instead of guard you. People who are more critical than complimentary. Have the ability to disconnect from unqualified people who decrease your life. Those who are critical than complimentary, those who belittle you and your dreams, those who humiliate and embarrass you, those who gossip, bicker, and backbite you.

Sometimes the most ordinary things could be made extraordinary, just by doing them with the right people. Get the right people in your life. I remember as a teenager, hanging around certain people I would always 100% of the time get into trouble. When my parents decided that that was my problem and they put a stop to who I spent time with, the trouble seemed to stop.

Who are the Right people? People who have success and experience in the area that you need help. People who have unconditional love for you. People who have good thinking skills. People who have nothing to gain by your choice. God gives us people to love and things to use, not things to love and people to use. Value the right people in your life. God sends people into our lives. How we treat them determines whether they stay. Joel Brown of The Addicted To Success podcast and website said, "Surround yourself with people who will transform your life, hold you to your greatest potential and are willing to tell you the truth no matter how hard it is."

I have gotten through some of the darkest, painful, and disappointing times in my life only because of who I was connected too. Real friends that did not leave my side in my toughest moments, but gathered around me, loved me, prayed for me, and encouraged me.

Life is filled with givers and takers. A person in your life who does not increase you will inevitably decrease you. You must discern the people in your life. You must decide how much time you are going to invest in others. You meet and become acquainted with many people in the course of your life, however, there are three levels in which we must recognize. Those three levels are: Relationship, Friendship, and Companionship.

Your past, present, and future is always connected to people. Relationships are founded on the discovery that you need people to be a success in life. They help us define who we are, what we can become, and where we want to be. We can trace all our successes to pivotal relationships. Where you want to be and where you want to go in life will be based on the books you read and the people you connect with.

Jesus, The world's foremost expert on relationships

Two things must Increase for relationships to move to the next level. An increase of quality of time and Increase of quality of shared information. Jesus said in John 15:13-15 NIV, *"Greater love has no one than this: to lay down one's life for one's friends. 14 You are my friends if you do what I command. 15 I no longer call you servants, because a servant does not know his master's business. Instead, I have called you friends, for everything that I learned from my Father I have made known to you."* "Laying down my life" is my TIME and "Everything I've made known to you" is INFORMATION. Giving those relationships your time is the utmost of importance. Life moves at the speed of connections. Schedule that breakfast or lunch. Make time for coffee. If they live far away, facetime with them regularly. Then share your heart and life. You can't expect others to read your mind. False expectations occur when we refuse to talk things out or be open and honest. Do not harbor or hide your hurts and disappointments that you are experiencing.

Relationships teach us that we were not created to succeed alone. Friendships teach us that real success is a shared destiny. In the book of Ecclesiastes 4:9-10 NIV it says, *"Two are better than one because they have a good return for their labor:10 If either of them falls, one can help the other up. But pity anyone who falls and has no one to help them up."* You must discern the people God has placed in your life to complete you. Jim Rohn said, "One person caring about another represents life's greatest value." Our relationships will always determine the direction and quality of our lives. With the right people in your corner, you become unstoppable! Who is in your corner? With whom are you connected?

Chapter 8

Wisdom: The Master Key To All The Treasures of Life

"The real measure of a man's wisdom is how much he would be worth if he lost all his money."

#robberbs

"The simple things are also the most extraordinary things, and only the wise can see them."

Paulo Coelho, The Alchemist #robberbs

"Listen to the words of the wise; apply your heart to my instruction.18 For it is good to keep these sayings in your heart and always ready on your lips."

Proverbs 22:17-18 NLT

One day Charlie Brown came home with his report card. As he turned on the television, his sister Lucy scoffed at his grade: "You got a "C" in history? That's only average." Charlie Brown defended himself: "So what? I'm an average student in an average school in an average community. What's wrong with being average?" Lucy retorted, "Because Charlie Brown you're capable of doing much better.

How many of us settle for just average? We are all capable of doing much better. Spiritually, socially, relationally, and financially. Improvement isn't automatic. You're only young once, but you can be ignorant indefinitely. Each year the lobster is forced to shed its shell; It is a pity we are not! Come on; If you do not make personal growth and improvement your responsibility, it will never happen. The road to anything worthwhile is always uphill, so the sooner you start climbing, the closer to reaching your God-ordained potential you will be.

Personal growth and improvement is our responsibility.

"For things to change, you have to change. For things to get better, you have to get better. For things to improve, you have to improve. When you grow, everything in your life grows with you." Jim Rohn

When you improve yourself spiritually, mentally, relationally, and financially, you improve your life. The word improve is defined as the act or process of making something better; increased value or excellence; advance, development, upgrade, refinement, renovation, enhancement, advancement, and upgrading. To make radical improvements in your life, you need either inspiration or desperation and definitely perspiration.

The sad thing is 95% of our society settles for far less than they want in this life, wishing they had more, living with regret, and never understanding that they could be, do, and have MORE out of life. Your life will get better when you get better!

What Do You Get from Failure? Wisdom

People naturally want more money, more time, more health, more wealth, more love, and more happiness. Regardless of your age or current situation in life, the only way to get there is one thing...wisdom. Wisdom is knowledge of what is true coupled with just judgment as to action; sagacity, discernment, or insight. The Hebrew word means "Skilled in Living." To know what to do with what you know is the essence of wisdom. The Law of God applied accurately to your life to solve problems.

Proverbs 4:5-8 in the Amplified Bible says, *"Get skillful and godly Wisdom, get understanding (discernment, comprehension, and interpretation); do not forget and do not turn back from the words of my mouth.6 Forsake not [Wisdom], and she will keep, defend, and protect you; love her, and she will guard you. 7 The beginning of Wisdom is: get Wisdom (skillful and godly Wisdom)! [For skillful and godly Wisdom is the principal thing.] And with all you have gotten, get understanding (discernment, comprehension, and interpretation). 8 Prize Wisdom highly and exalt her, and she will exalt and promote you; she will bring you to honor when you embrace her."* Today there is lots of knowledge, but little understanding. Lots of means, but little meaning. Many know how, but little know why. Lots of sights, but little of insight. Can you think of anything worse than living a life devoid of growth and improvement?

We are all born ignorant, but one must work hard to remain stupid. - Benjamin Franklin

Wisdom is the master key to all the treasures of life. The word Treasure is defined as wealth, rich materials, or valuable things. Any thing or person greatly valued or highly prized: to value, esteem. Solomon was born around 974 BC. He became

King at 12 yrs old, was the wealthiest man who ever lived. He actually was a Trillionaire in today's income. Why? He asked for Wisdom. 2 Chronicles 1:10-12 NIV - *Give me wisdom and knowledge, that I may lead this people, for who is able to govern this great people of yours?"11 God said to Solomon, "Since this is your heart's desire, and you have not asked for wealth, possessions or honor, nor for the death of your enemies, and since you have not asked for a long life but for wisdom and knowledge to govern my people over whom I have made you king, 12 therefore, wisdom and knowledge will be given you. And I will also give you wealth, possessions and honor, such as no king who was before you ever had, and none after you will have."*

Solomon said that wisdom is more precious than rubies, and nothing you desire can compare with her. (Proverbs 8:11) The highest quality ruby is 10x more valuable than a top diamond - 1 gram of gold= $50 - 1 gram precious ruby=$50,000! He said in Proverbs 16:16 NIV - *"How much better to get wisdom than gold, to get insight rather than silver!"* The gold reserves worth hundreds of billions of dollars. 4000 stalls for his horses and chariots. 12,000 horseman on his payroll. Ruler of nations sought his advice and paid him for it.

If God offered you One Thing what would it be?

Solomon said in Proverbs 2:1-4 NIV - *"My son, if you accept my words and store up my commands within you, 2 turning your ear to wisdom and applying your heart to understanding—3 indeed, if you call out for insight and cry aloud for understanding, 4 and if you look for it as for silver and search for it as for hidden treasure,"* You always INVEST in what you find valuable. Invest in wisdom! If you think investing in yourself is expensive, you should try ignorance.

Proverbs 1:5 NIV - *Let the wise listen and add to their learning, and let the discerning get guidance*

Don't be a know it all. Be a learn it all! Don't bankrupt your mind. Warren Buffet said the most important investment you can make is in yourself. The highest value in life is not what you get but what you become! When you improve yourself, you improve your life! No one gets paid by the hour for a job; we get paid for the value we provide within that hour. Make yourself valuable and you will increase your income.

Buy the books, go to the seminars, continue to learn, and purchase the audios and videos. GROW GROW GROW! Are the products worth it? I don't know, but YOU ARE. A university study done a few years ago found that almost one-third of all professionals were so busy working, they were two years behind in the latest developments in their field. If you want to be a continual learner, you must carve out time to do it! Henry Ford said, "It's been my observation that successful people get ahead during the time other people waste." Never leave your Bible, books (kindle), podcasts when you travel. Seize every opportunity to keep growing, attend "Automobile University." Warren Buffet said the most important investment you can make is in yourself.

The secret to becoming a learner is to learn something new every day! Listen, "Get understanding. Esteem her, and she will exalt you." Proverbs 22:17-18 NLT says — *"Listen to the words of the wise; apply your heart to my instruction.18 For it is good to keep these sayings in your heart and always ready on your lips."* Coach John Wooden once said, "What counts, is what you learn after you know it all." That's because the more you learn, the less you think you have to learn. You are never too old to learn to be wise! If you are alive, you are never too young.

A Proverb a Day Builds Wisdom

In my estimation, of the Bible's 66 Books, Proverbs is the most provocative. If it is true that good judgment is caught, not taught, then Proverbs drops pearls. More than two dozen centuries before Sigmund Freud and Psychological profiling, this set of 31 chapters outstripped human understanding with insight into sex, anger management, slander, wealth, welfare, business ethics, intoxication, pride, and subtle human fissures as relevant as today and tomorrows blogs. Read one chapter of Proverbs a day, and I promise you, wisdom will come into your life.

When you read, meditate, and memorize a book like the Bible on a daily basis. It injects your entire being with wisdom. Proverbs 2:6-7 NIV says, *"For the Lord gives wisdom; from his mouth come knowledge and understanding. He holds success in store for the upright, He is a shield to those whose walk is blameless."* I would encourage you to not be closed minded to the Bible. It is like Mark Twain said, "It ain't those parts of the Bible that I can't understand that bother me, it is the parts that I do understand." People do not reject the Bible because it contradicts itself but because it contradicts them.

The Bible is powerful. The principles that we need to know about success, wealth, relationships, business, and happiness are contained within the binding of one book, the Bible. Within it, you will find the answer to all of life's problems and opportunities. Napoleon Bonaparte said, "The Bible is no mere book, but a living creature, with a power that conquers all who oppose it." If you take the principles of the Bible and apply it to your life, success will leap from the pages and become a reality in your life. Written are ancient and relevant wisdom. Utterly applicable to your life, relationship, and business. All

66 Books, 1,189 Chapters, 31,273 verses are God-breathed and life-giving.

When you Increase Your Wisdom You Will Increase Your Wealth

Ben Franklin once said, "Empty the money of your wallet into your mind, and your mind will fill your wallet with money." Solomon tells us throughout Proverbs to seek wisdom as if it were the hidden treasure. True wisdom is rarely found lying on the ground in plain view. Instead, it is a treasure that must be searched out, and those seeking it must often dig beneath the surface. But it is not a challenging pursuit. It is fun to search for buried treasure, and it is wonderfully rewarding to find it.

Psalm 112:1-3 NIV says, *Praise the Lord.[b] Blessed are those who fear the Lord, who find great delight in his commands. Their children will be mighty in the land; the generation of the upright will be blessed. 3 Wealth and riches are in their houses, and their righteousness endures forever.* And Proverbs 3:16 NIV says *"Long life is in her right hand; in her left hand are riches and honor."*

Wealth is not just having to deal with the accumulation of money. Wealth is knowledge, confidence, and attitude. It is the security that comes from the experience that no matter what happens in your life and finances, you have the power and ability to change your thinking, your beliefs, your words, your actions, and your strategies to turn your situation around.

When you have wisdom, you can lose your cash, savings, credit, retirement, and even investments. The one thing that will get all that back and rebuild your wealth is wisdom. Wealth, success, and money is the tangible evidence and result of wisdom. Get wisdom, and you can get everything else you want and need in this life.

Wisdom + Financial Failure = Success

I have succeeded financially, and I have failed financially. I have made a lot of money, saved money, invested money, and lost money. In 2008 when the market tanked, my wife and I had money in real estate investments and mutual funds. Of course, along with a job transition and relocation, we hit financial trouble. We had no other choice but to file bankruptcy in 2011.

Bradley Klontz, a clinical psychologist in Hawaii, is a co-author of "The Financial Wisdom of Ebenezer Scrooge: 5 Principles to Transform Your Relationship with Money," and said that bankruptcy can affect mental health. "Bankruptcy is an enormous financial and psychological stressor," Klontz said in an e-mail. "Financial stress can lead to a loss of personal control, depression, anxiety, shame and relationship problems."

Many people put too much emphasis on money, so that is why suffering can result from bankruptcy. "Many of us confuse our self-worth with our net-worth," Klontz said. "As such, financial problems can deal devastating blows to our self-esteem. Bankruptcy can lead to feelings of guilt and shame, and cause us to isolate from our family and friends out of embarrassment."

Bankruptcy hurts because it is viewed as a personal financial failure with a few doses of guilt and shame. In 2011, 1.37 million people filed. You may be reading this, and you have never had to do file bankruptcy. Well just imagine how we felt. The guilt. The condemnation. The shame that comes along with it. Your name is published in the newspaper of the city you file. Over the years, one of the most commonly repeated statements

I hear from people is how they feel guilty or ashamed that they have gotten themselves into their current position. Needless to say, the filing was quite overwhelming but also a relief.

I am telling this because you may have hit rock bottom financially. If you have, I am writing this to let you know that with wisdom you can recover, restore, and rebuild your life, wealth, and finances. Though financial matters are often seen as cold, calculating or rational, the reality is that emotions are often interwoven with many money decisions. This is never truer than when discussing filing for bankruptcy. Though it may seem like a clear-cut financial question, a matter of dollars and cents, these decisions can result in tremendous anxiety, guilt and even shame. Many people feel guilty about considering filing for bankruptcy and begin to believe they are trapped by the misconduct.

Did you know that some of the most brilliant and successful people in our history filed bankruptcy. Here is a list of people you may have known or read about who filed bankruptcy and failed financially. Thomas Jefferson, 3rd US President, Abraham Lincoln, 16th US President, Harry S. Truman, 35th President, John Wayne, Hollywood Film Legend, Daniel Boone, American frontiersman, Larry King, TV Talk Show Star, Gloria Vanderbilt, Clothes designer, Marvin Gaye, American Singer, MC Hammer, Grammy Winning Rapper, Jerry Lee Lewis, Willie Nelson, Wayne Newton, and Tom Petty. Frank Baum, author of The Wizard of Oz, Mark Twain, Oscar Wilde, and even Frank Lloyd Wright. Actors Redd Foxx, Judy Garland, Jerry Lewis, and Burt Reynolds. How about moguls of finance who filed. PT Barnum, Founder of Barnum & Bailey Circus, Francis Ford Coppola, who directed the Godfather, Walt Disney, Henry Ford, Paulo Gucci, H.J. Heinz, Conrad Hilton, Charles Schwab, Sam Walton, and even our current President, Donald Trump. The list goes on and on and on.

OK, so you may be asking what happened next. It was simple. None of us have a money problem we have a wisdom problem. If we get wisdom, we get our answers. I began a journey to get wisdom on how to bounce back after bankruptcy.

How to completely recover from financial failure.

Three books that were great assets and helped to downloaded a wealth of wisdom for my family and me. Napoleon Hill's Think and Grow Rich, Success The Glenn Bland Method by Glenn Bland, and Credit After Bankruptcy by Stephen Snyder. One can purchase these books on amazon.com.

Stephen Snyder was my brother-in-law. His book was a best seller and he and my sister-in-law, Michele, traveled all over the United States giving free seminars based on the wealth and wisdom in the book. They were able and helped thousands of people recover from bankruptcy. Stephen was featured many times on Fox, CNN, ABC, CNBC, and the Wall Street Journal.

After attending the seminar, reading the entire book, my wife, Tricia, and I began to apply the wisdom to rebuild our credit, credit score, and finances. You can go to www.lifeafter-bankruptcy.com to learn how to use the principles and recover your wealth. All you need is wisdom. Today we both have an A1 credit rating, money in savings, own our own home and have increased our investments and retirement.

Wisdom enables you to overcome significant obstacles and opposition. It helps you work smarter, not harder. It even gives you favor. Wisdom creates an atmosphere for wealth. Wealth cannot create an atmosphere for wisdom. Wisdom creates an atmosphere for wealth. It is not money you need, but it is wisdom. If you lack wealth or anything, ask God for wisdom!

Chapter 9

Forgiveness: Everyone Wins

"The weak can never forgive. Forgiveness is the attribute of the strong."

Mahatma Gandhi #robberbs

"Then Peter came to him and asked, "Lord, how often should I forgive someone who sins against me? Seven times?" "No, not seven times," Jesus replied, "but seventy times seven."

Matthew 18:21-22 NLT

"When you forgive, you in no way change the past - but you sure do change the future."

Bernard Meltzer #robberbs

Why a chapter on forgiveness? Because many of your failings, fallings, and getting knocked down are caused by other individuals. Holding on to bitterness, anger, strife, and unforgiveness will keep you down. The bottom line is that you have to learn to forgive and let go so you can get back up and move forward. Living your life, mastering your vision and goals, and even manifesting your dreams will require you to let go of what holds you back. The momentum that will drive you to succeed takes the confidence and power to let go of these diseases and release those people. The release is driven by the difficulty to forgive and move on.

You have the human need to hold someone accountable for how you feel, or what happened to you. You think you need to assign fault or make someone wrong to find some kind of closure to your circumstance. Whenever you place the responsibility for your feelings or situations on someone or something else, you will never get closure. Forgiveness is just the process of releasing your feelings of resentment, hurt, and anger which you hold against another person or persons, or an event. When you decide to forgive, it brings you to a place of peace where you will no longer demand restitution, restoration, retribution, or revenge. Forgiveness is the starting point where you can get back up, move forward, and start the process of winning in this life.

Relinquish Your Right To Get Even

Paul the Apostle was very clear in Romans 12:19 (NIV) when he said, *"Do not take revenge, my friends..."* Today we love to do the opposite. We like to take matters into our own hands. We love to get on our social media channels and publish our hurt, or our revenge. Hurt people always hurt people.

Charles Dickens had an incredible way of creating such memorable characters in his beloved novels. Tiny Tim, Ebenezer Scrooge, Bob Cratchit, Bob Marley, Oliver Twist, David Copperfield, Uriah Heap, Lucy Minette, and every other unbelievable character. The character I want to focus on right now is the maddening, pathetic, unforgettable woman he named Miss Havisham.

If you have never read Great Expectations, let me give you a little background. Miss Havisham was a wealthy young woman who was happily engaged to a young man. But on the morning of her wedding day, as she was dressing for the ceremony, at exactly twenty minutes to nine, she received a devastating message from her fiancé, totally jilting her and stopping her dead in her tracts. Here is what she then did. The moment she received the news of her disappointment she stopped all the clocks in her house, twenty minutes to nine, and never to run again. She closed all the drapes en-sure day-light would never enter as long as she lived. She already put on her wedding dress, and for the rest of her life, she would never remove it. She had one wedding shoe on and was about to put on the other. So she hobbled about with one shoe on and one shoe off the rest of her life. The wedding cake was placed on the table, and she vowed no one to re-move it for the rest of her life.

Miss Havisham's behavior is not healthy. It seems almost unrealistic. But it is realistic because this happens to you emo-tionally, internally, mentally, in your feelings and attitudes when you are devastated in some way. Like Scrooge represents stinginess, Oliver Twist represents neglect, and Tiny Tim rep-resents overcoming a handicap, Miss Havisham represents a living, breathing, personification of rejection. Why? You have been rejected, disappointed, and hurt in some way or another. Do you behave as she did? Do you stop the clocks, draw all the drapes, wear the same clothes? No. But you do withdraw. The hurt is sometimes so painful you cannot move on. You are paralyzed. You hide under facades. You change your attitude to be something fierce and negative. You get depressed. You do not want to be around other people. It is all you ever talk about. The pain, the event, the circumstance consumes you.

You want to hurt the person who hurt you more. Dickens teaches that you can never avenge yourselves on someone who does not care about you. Miss Havisham wasted her entire life in revenge and it was the most narcissistic thing she should have done. Do not allow someone else's actions, determine your outcome. No matter what has been done to you. I Peter 2:23 LB said, *"When Jesus suffered, He did not threaten to get even; He left His case in the hands of God...* Dickens teaches us that by Miss Havisham's sad ending that this is not what you should do. Leave things in the hands of God. She did not, and she lived her life as a lie, a sham. She was "Have a sham." You must remember, Somebody needs your forgiveness more than you need to be vindicated.

Forgiveness really is "Letting It Go"

RT Kendall said, "When everything in you wants to hold a grudge, point the finger, and remember the pain, God wants you to lay it all aside." You need to let it go! I know you love to think about what those people did to you. You get churned up inside. You like to repeat the pain time and time again. You have to forgive and let forgiveness reign in your life. If not, you will have no peace. Quit nursing the attitude of unforgiveness. You only damage yourself. The person who gains the most from forgiveness is the person who does the forgiving.

Take President Nelson Mandela for example. He experienced 27 years of political incarceration. The longest-serving political prisoner in the world. But he emerged out of prison unscathed and told his people of South Africa to forgive their oppressors and focus on the future and building a newly united nation. In spite of the devastating trauma of apartheid, President Mandela chose the path of forgiveness and reconciliation rather than the policy of revenge and vindictiveness.

The Apostle Paul was very clear and direct when he said in Ephesians 4:32 (NIV), *"Be kind and compassionate to one another, forgiving one another, just as Christ has forgave you. "* Then he went on to repeat it in Colossians 3:13 (NIV), *"Bear with each other and forgive whatever grievances you may have against one another. Forgive as the Lord forgave you."* You will live your life with complete peace of mind, peace with people, and peace with God if you walk in forgiveness and forgive the people who knocked you down. Dr. Norman Cousins said, "Life is an adventure in forgiveness." It takes guts to forgive. In thirty years of ministry and being a pastor I have worked diligently to walk this out. When dealing with people, there is always times of pain, hurt, rejection, and disappointment. I have experienced all of these great pains. People whom I gave my life, time, and even money too. People whom I did life together. Whom I was very close. I was with them in their darkest times and times of celebration. I prayed with them, cried with them, ate dinner with them, and laughed with them. Only for them to find something they did not like about me, my decisions, my leadership, my messages, etc…to turn on me, reject my family, and our church and then leave. A pastor feels utter rejection when someone leaves their church and always takes it personally. These people not only go but spread toxic poisons to other individuals in the church and next thing you know many are gone. I coach pastors and leaders on a monthly basis in dealing with this disappointment. I encourage them, like Nelson Mandela, to be quick to forgive, so it does not cause them to be bitter and overwhelm them. The key is to concentrate not on what is lost, but what is left. Focus on being a reaching culture, not just a keeping culture.

Forgiveness is The Heart of The Matter

One of my favorite songs is by Don Henley called, "The Heart of the Matter," which is a part of his "The End of Innocence" album. The song is about forgiveness. Forgiveness is one of the hardest human emotions, particularly when it comes to someone we love or even detest. It opens up with strong guitar chords. Then Henley begins to sing in his amazing voice about a relationship that soured and a girlfriend who found someone else: His pleading voice sings..."I'm learning to live without you now, But I miss you sometimes, and the more I know, the less I understand....But I think it's about forgiveness, forgiveness, even if, even if you don't love me anymore." He is not asking for forgiveness, but he is letting her know I choose to forgive. He made the decision. Forgiveness is never a feeling, but it is always a decision. Forgiveness is a decision to release a person from the obligation that resulted when he or she injured you.

To face life's challenges or adversities, you must maintain forward motion in your life. This will cause you to remain steadfast on your path to purpose, victory, and success. You will be able to get up, master your goals, and even manifest your dreams. Forgiveness allows you to release the past hurts, injuries, and rejections and continue to advance in the direction of moving forward. There is nothing you can do to change your yesterday. Paul said in Philippians 3:13-14 (NIV), *"Forgetting what is behind and straining toward what is ahead, I press on toward the goal to win the prize for which God has called me."*

Forgiveness may not ever change the past, but it can change your future. Remember unforgiveness and bitterness is a danger to your life, health, wealth, and relationships. It will eat you from the inside out. It will go everywhere with you. God did not give you the capacity to carry this weight in your life. What if you would merely absorb each other's pain in life? What if you would be more caring and comforting to each other rather than critical and condescending?

Today, I encourage you to rise from the ashes, the burdens, the rejections, and the pains of the past. Forgive those who have hurt you, but also forgive yourself. Let go of what once was, so you can create and enjoy what is and what will be. Did you know that to be free you need to forgive others? Every time you make someone wrong and hold grievance toward them, being the judge of their bad behavior, you are metaphorically putting them in prison. And guess who has to stand guard at that prison? You do! How can you be truly free if you are busy guarding that prison you made for them? So today, within your own mind and heart choose to forgive for one reason... so you can be FREE. When you forgive, everyone wins!

Chapter 10

The Ultimate Comeback Produces the Ultimate Life

"I think its possible for ordinary people to choose to be extraordinary."

Elon Musk #robberbs

"The rest of my life will be the best of my life"

Dr. Dave Martin #robberbs

"The Lord will make you the head, not the tail. If you pay attention to the commands of the Lord your God that I give you this day and carefully follow them, you will always be at the top, never at the bottom."

Deuteronomy 28:13 (NIV)

In a Charles Schultz "Peanuts" cartoon, Lucy comes up to Charlie Brown and says, "You know, life is like an ocean liner. Some people take their deck chair and put it on the stern, to see where they have been. And some people put their deck chair on the bow, to see where they are going. Charlie Brown, tell me, "Where do you want to put your deck chair?" Perplexed momentarily, Charlie Brown looks at Lucy and says, "I don't know. I can't even unfold my deck chair."

Are you tired of living at the bottom when everyone around you seems to be rising to higher places? Some principles will help you achieve the ultimate life that you desire. No more barely getting by, no more bottom of the barrel thinking, and no more staying down. Whether it is in your finances, your relationships, thoughts in your mind or desires in your heart. There is a more prosperous, fuller and more rewarding life in store for you if you apply these principles. It is time to rise, shake off the old ways and make a quality decision to do whatever it takes to live the ultimate life! The word "ultimate" is defined as "the best achievable or imaginable of its kind. the best or most extreme of its kind."

You Were Created to live an Extraordinary Life

It says in Genesis 1 verse 28, *"God blessed them and said to them, "Be fruitful and increase in number; fill the earth and subdue it. Rule over the fish in the sea and the birds in the sky and over every living creature that moves on the ground."* God made everything, and He declared it good. God's plan was He made man to be blessed and have a prosperous, abundant life. Life is meant to be good. It was His contract with humans. When God said, "Be Fruitful" He meant "always producing," to be productive in the world. "Multiply" meant "always increasing", made to be prosperous, abundant, more than what you already have. "Replenish," always fill and refill. Use and consume, but you are obligated by God to restock, refill, and replace what you have used. "Sub-due," control your environment. If you don't control your environment, your environment will control you. These are not only these promises but solutions for us to exemplify.

In Deuteronomy 28:13 (NIV) Moses said to the people, *"The Lord will make you the head, not the tail. If you pay attention to the commands of the Lord your God that I give you this day and carefully follow them, you will always be at the top, never at the bottom."* He was reminding them of the life they were to live. An ultimate life. An extraordinary life. This moves on even into the new testament with the message of Jesus. He said in John 10:10 (ESV), *"The thief comes only to steal and kill and destroy. I came that they may have life and have it abundantly."* Jesus is declaring His intention to recover and restore God's original intent for us. The word "abundant" actually means "existing or available in large quantities; plentiful, excessive, profuse, rich, lavish, abounding, liberal, generous, bountiful, large, huge, great, paramount, overflowing, prolific, extraordinary."

There is More. Do not Settle!

How many of you settle for just whatever kind of life? Sad thing is 95% of people settle for far less than they want in this life, wishing they had more, living with regret, and never understanding that they could be, do, and have MORE out of life. Do these seem like empty promises to you and that God is merely baiting you to get your attention or do you believe that God can help you live the ultimate life? Are you experiencing all that God wants for you? You need to realize and believe that you can live the ultimate, abundant, and prosperous life.

During the days of Christopher Columbus, Spain was very proud of the fact that they were the last point of solid land for sailors going westward. When travelers arrived, there was a large sign that said their motto in Latin, "Ne Plus Ultra" which means " No more beyond." It was on their flag and coins as well. Their outlook on life was "No more beyond." It was the world as they knew it. Their result was they settled. People settled there because they were told there is nothing beyond Spain.

After Columbus discovered the New World - the national motto for Spain changed to "Plus Ultra" which means "MORE BEYOND" they dropped "Ne." Sadly, Many people have settled for their version of Spain. Have you stopped dreaming, hoping, believing, and praying? Some people accept something far less than God's more significant, grander plans for their lives. Don't settle. Realize you can have, experience, and live the ultimate life.

It Takes Vision to Live the Ultimate Life

Jeremiah 29:11 NIV says *"For I know the plans I have for you,"* declares the Lord, *"Plans to prosper you and not to harm you, plans to give you hope and a future."* Life is a journey, and every journey has a destination. Everybody ends up somewhere in life. A few people end up somewhere on purpose. A vision gets you where you need to go.

What is vision? Webster's definition is The ability to force or perceive something not actually visible, as though mental or spiritual acuteness. A vision is a compelling image of a possible future - Vision brings your world into focus. It brings order to chaos. A clear vision enables you to see everything differently. It is born in the soul of a man or woman who is consumed with the tension between what is and what could be. Anyone who is frustrated, or brokenhearted about the way things are, in light of the way they believe things could be, is a candidate for vision.

Get a vision for your life that makes you want to jump out of bed in the morning! Why? Because you will never go beyond where you see yourself going. The World is just waiting for you to....Get a VISION of your life that is so big the hair on the back of your neck will stand up! Get a VISION so awesome that your toes curl! Get a VISION so big that 100 years from now, future generations birthed from you will look at your picture and say, "Thank you!"

Proverbs 29:18 KJV says, *"Where there is no vision, the people perish: but he that keepeth the law, happy is he."* Where there is no vision for an extraordinary ultimate life, people will perish, and where there is a vision people flourish and live an ultimate life. Yogi Berra said, "If you don't know where you are going, you're likely to end up someplace else."

When it comes to vision there are two common conditions: Farsighted is a focus on things that are distant and nearsighted is a focus on things that are close. Some have excellent vision, and others do not. Some of you are farsighted, where you have envisioned the future, but lack the day to day disciplines to get you there. Some are near-sighted, and you know what to do today, but not sure where you are headed. Wayne Gretzky was asked why he was the world's greatest hockey player at the time. He replied, "While most hockey players go to where the hockey puck is, I always go to where I see the hockey puck will be." By having a grand vision for your life, you can see where you want to be and move in that direction.

Vision is a picture. Anytime there is no VISION, the quality and value of life deteriorate. A marriage, a business, an organization, a company, a city, a nation, or a school will fall apart when they lack VISION. No vision for marriage ends up in divorce. No vision for financial freedom even if you want prosperity will come up in scarcity and poverty. No vision for health even you can want to be in shape and have 6-pack abs, but you will end up getting a keg.

Legendary golfer Jack Nicklaus once said, "I never hit a shot, not even in practice, without having a very sharp infocus picture of it in my head." A lack of vision will trap you in the normal rotation of mediocrity that results in a life of regrets and disappointments. Get a vision for your life that makes you want to jump out of bed in the morning! Why? Because you will never go beyond where you see yourself going. Oprah Winfrey said, "Create the highest, grandest vision possible for your life because you become what you believe." Helen Keller once said, "It's a terrible thing to see, and have no vision!" Keller believed that we need to have a direction and a grand vision for ourselves. It is important to envision the future and imagine who we want to be, where we want to go and what kind of life we want to lead. If we can see it in our mind, we can hold it in our hand. We can indeed live and experience the ultimate life.

It is Like Alice in Wonderland where Alice comes to the junction in the road that leads in different directions. She does not know where she wants to go, so she asks the Cheshire Cat for advice: "Cheshire Cat....Would you tell me please, which way I ought to go from here?" "That depends a good deal on where you want to get to," the Cat said. "I don't care much where..." Alice said. "Then it doesn't matter which way you go," the Cat said. Don't be like Alice! Begin right now to decide exactly where you want to go!

What You See is What You Get

Life without a vision is a life that goes nowhere. A visionless life is continuously trapped in the regular rotation of mediocrity that will always result in regrets, loss, failure, defeats, and disappointments. Our vision is empowered by what we see, our imagination, pictures in front of us. Those always win over logic. Vision supersedes the facts. It makes what facts change to reality. What do you see? What is your vision? Can you imagine yourself living the ultimate life?

Focus on thinking positive thoughts, visualizing successful outcomes, taking action, to experience better results in your life. #robberbs

Many times you do not possess the things you envision because you lack the faith, the expectation and capacity to see the possibility to see it come to pass. Frank Gaines said, "Only he who can see the invisible can do the impossible." Listen, if you can see it, you can have it. Visions become a reality. In the Old Testament, God spoke to Abraham and told him in Genesis 22:17 NIV - *"I will surely bless you and make your descendants as numerous as the stars in the sky and as the sand on the seashore. Your descendants will take possession of the cities of their enemies,"* Even though Abraham and Sarah had no children, God gave him a vision that he was to focus on and look at regardless of his present condition. When you see the vision, you realize your current situation is not your final destination. His vision came to pass. He became the patriarch of the three largest religions in the world.

God brought clarity to Abraham's dream through the use of a Picture - This relieves the tension between his faith in the promise and the present realities. In Genesis 15:5 NIV - He took him outside and said, *"Look up at the sky and count the stars—if indeed you can count them." Then he said to him, "So shall your offspring[a] be."* God used the IMAGERY of stars and sand to help strengthen the dream in his heart that was growing weak due to the negative impact of temporary circumstances.

Thucydides said, " The bravest are surely those who have the clearest vision of what is before them, glory and danger alike, and yet notwithstanding go out to meet it." What is your vision for your life? Write it down in your journal. What is the vision for your family? Write it down. A short pencil is better than a long memory. If you see it, envision it, then ink it. What's the vision for your business or career? Write it down. We are only limited by our vision or imagination.

Get a Vision Board

Since the release of the 2006 book (and film) The Secret, vision boards have grown in popularity. A vision board is a collage of visual images or words that represent the life you want to live. Your imagination is an invisible machine inside your mind. God gave it to you to create pictures. Pictures of what you dream about and desire.

Quite literally, it is a tangible representation of the vision you have for yourself. You can make one by hand—think old-school magazine cutouts on a bulletin board—or you can make one digitally, via a website like Pinterest. What matters is that you manually create it (no one else can do it for you) and that it excites you when you see it. It can represent your vision for a particular area of your life (i.e., your career), or your whole life in general. So a few years ago I went to the store and bought all my kids, Cierra, Christian, Grayson, Emily and Evan, including myself, vision boards. Vision boards help us to stay focused. We have pictures of things we want to achieve, places we want to go, money we want to make, cars we want to drive, and things we want to experience.

That vision board is a powerful tool that helps you narrow down your desires, dreams, and vision, whatever is in your heart or mind. The tool enables you to invest the time and energy to visualize your future and consistently reminds you of your life goals. Jack Canfield said, "Your brain will work tirelessly to achieve the statements you give your subconscious mind. And when those statements are the affirmations and images of your goals, you are destined to achieve them!" He went on to say, By putting a vision board somewhere you can see it every day, you will prompt yourself to visualize your ideal life on a regular basis. And that is important because visualization activates the creative powers of your subconscious mind and programs your brain to notice available resources that were always there but escaped your notice. The Minor Prophet Habakkuk said, (2:2) "Then the LORD told me: *"I will give you my message in the form of a vision. Write it clearly enough to be read at a glance."* I am able to look at mine numerous times a day and because of that some of those visions have already come to pass.

Visions and Dreams Can Come True

I love Disney World; it is the happiest place on earth. It does not matter how many times I have been there. It is always like my first time. At its grand opening in October of 1971, at the festivities of this "land of fairy tales," the master of ceremonies turned to Walt's wife, Lillian, who was sitting in the audience. He asked her if she wished Walt could have witnessed this marvelous day, a testament to his vision, ingenuity, and hard work. Lillian said something surprising. She nodded and told him that Walt did. He had vision long before its grand opening. The only reason it opened was that Walt had an idea. No matter what his setbacks were, he kept the vision.

Every dream, every vision, and every idea begins on the inside of you, in your imagination, before it ever shows up on the outside. You have to have a vision for more than what is happening in your life. Albert Einstein said, "Your imagination is everything. It is simply the preview of life's coming attractions." When you go to the movies, you begin the adventure by watching the previews, or the highlights, of other films. A preview is anything that gives "an advance idea or impression of something to come." Your vision is designed to give you a picture of your future.

Great achievers learn to replay the memories of their past triumphs and preplay the vision of their desired successes. When David faced the giant Goliath, he mentally replayed his previous victories in killing the bear and the lion. Then he used his imagination to picture and preplay his impending victory over Goliath. Look at his vision and picture for slaying Goliath that would be given to him found in I Samuel 17:25-27 NIV - *"Now the Israelites had been saying, "Do you see how this man keeps coming out? He comes out to defy Israel. The king will give great wealth to the man who kills him. He will also give him his daughter in marriage and will exempt his family from taxes in Israel."26 David asked the men standing near him, "What will be done for the man who kills this Philistine and removes this disgrace from Israel? Who is this uncircumcised Philistine that he should defy the armies of the living God?" 27 They repeated to him what they had been saying and told him, "This is what will be done for the man who kills him."*

David saw the money, and he saw the honey! If you see what you want, You will get what you want. You are going to have to live in the future anyway, so it might as well be the future you are picturing for yourself, rather than a future that somebody else is designing for you. In your mind, you can go back to your past, or you can go to your future. You decide. Your mind is not restricted by location. God gave you a mind, so He can give you a picture of where He wants to take you. Where do you want to go from here? The past no longer matters. Your failure is not you. This is your time!

Will you leave your pain in the past to follow your dreams, or will you let these hurts steal your hope for a better life? Will you get up! Step out of the dominant culture of resignation and mediocrity and endeavor to create the experience of your visions and dreams! We have been programmed to live within the limitations that other people have set for us. I want to elevate our perception of what is possible for us. Solomon said in Proverbs 13:12 NKJV - *"Hope deferred makes the heart sick, But when the desire comes, it is a tree of life."*

Do not let anything hold you back. This is your ultimate comeback. Do not let anyone keep you from living this ultimate life. The visions God has given you are treasures worth living. Get up! Move on! Go to the next level! A person with a vision is more powerful then a person with all the facts. Remember, one bad chapter does not mean your story is over. Turn the page and start a new chapter! This is Your Ultimate Comeback!

About the Author

Rob Yanok is an Inspirational Speaker, Entrepreneur, Success Coach, and Author of "Divine Strategies for Success: Biblical Principles for Success at Life", "Your Ultimate Comeback (How To Get Up When Life Knocks You Down)", and his personal development system, "The Success at Life System: Strategies for Creating a Extraordinary Successful Life, 31 Life Changing sessions Recorded Live. He is an inspirational and motivational speaker and He serves as a Self development and organizational coach to many top achievers. He and his wife Tricia founded GraceTown in 2011 in Columbus, OH, which provided spiritual insight and direction for people of diverse ages, backgrounds, and needs. Rob has been speaking full-time since 1990.

Rob leads Robberbs International, a leading edge transformational, personal and spiritual development organization helping people and organizations around the world achieve and live an extraordinary life. Rob is a catalyst for change and a strategist for success. He helps ordinary people understand the significance of thinking and living successfully in every area of life. His messages are designed to empower people to rise above the most difficult challenges of life.

He has inspired thousands of people, sharing his breakthrough strategies on how to overcome adversity, achieve abundance and extraordinary success. He is a part of the Joel Osteen's Champions Network and sits on the board of some thriving churches and community organizations. Rob and Tricia enjoy living their life in New Albany, Ohio with their family, Cierra (and son in law Josh Rider), Christian, Grayson, Emily and Evan. They have two dogs, a Yorkshire terrier named Buckeye and a Labradoodle named Onyx.

Connect with Rob

www.robyanok.com
email: rob@robyanok.com

facebook
www.facebook.com/robyanok

twitter
www.twitter.com/robyanok

Instagram
www.instagram.com/robyanok

YouTube
www.youtube.com/robyanok

Linkedin
www.linkedin.com/robyanok

#robberbs #yourultimatecomeback #motivationsformonday

"Rob Yanok is a great friend and one of the most dynamic speakers that I know. His message of hope, possibility, and success will bring extraordinary increase to your life, church, conference, and organization. I want to encourage you when you are looking for a speaker, call my friend Rob Yanok. I promise you will be extremely satisfied and glad you did."

**Dr. Dave Martin,
President & CEO of Dave Martin Int'l**

To Schedule Rob to speak at your Church, Company, Association, or Organization:

Call 614. 636.1086
Visit us online at www.robyanok.com
email: rob@robyanok.com

50618120R00072

Made in the USA
Columbia, SC
09 February 2019